Praise for *How to Work wi*

"My favourite thing about Michael Bungay Stanier's work is his ability to deliver actionable, tactical strategies that are based on well-researched ideas and data, then packaged in a book that I can read on a flight. And the wisdom is real—it sticks. I haven't stopped thinking about 'Best Possible Relationships' and 'Keystone Conversations.'"
BRENÉ BROWN, PhD, *New York Times*–bestselling author of *Atlas of the Heart* and *Dare to Lead*

"This little volume has actionable advice on every page, and it's a fun read, too."
AMY EDMONDSON, Professor at Harvard Business School and author of *The Fearless Organization*

"A modern classic, this book will save relationships, careers, and organizations."
SETH GODIN, author of *The Song of Significance*

"Here is a practical, tactical guide to help you rebuild the most human of skills: conversation. Essential!"
KIM SCOTT, author of *Radical Candor* and *Just Work*

"Michael Bungay Stanier's genius for making the complex simple is on full display. Bravo!"
WHITNEY JOHNSON, *Wall Street Journal*–bestselling author of *Smart Growth*

"Michael Bungay Stanier's practical guide to cultivating Keystone Conversations can unlock the full potential of an individual, and that of the wider team."
LOREN I. SHUSTER, Chief People Officer and Head of Corporate Affairs at The LEGO Group

"This deep book will show you how to build brilliant relationships even in difficult times. Reading it made me feel like I could work with anyone. You will too."
LIZ WISEMAN, *New York Times*–bestselling author of *Multipliers* and *Impact Players*

"This book simplifies the complex processes of starting, improving, and maintaining our best possible connections."
BRUCE W. PARKER, Chief Sales Officer at Deloitte Canada

"The Keystone Conversation Michael Bungay Stanier teaches us is the framework I've been seeking to help leaders begin any relationship better."
DAVE STACHOWIAK, Host of the *Coaching for Leaders* podcast

"This exceptional book provides the practical tools and self-reflections that will help you gain critical insights in how to approach any conversation successfully."
STEFANI OKAMOTO, Director of Global Learning & Development at Microsoft

The quality of your working relationships determines your success and your happiness.
Stop leaving it to chance.
Start building the best possible relationships.

Michael Bungay Stanier
(It's a bit of a mouthful of a name, which is why many people call me MBS.)

The crazy ones, the misfits, the re

ones, the bossy, the picky, the

peacemakers, the changemaker

the lead guitar, the rhythm sect

certain, the confused, lain fro

Resources, the fighters, the fligl

leaders, the followers, the ove

geeky, the grumpy, the dopey,

the mumblers, the oldtimers, th

e delightful ones, the frustrating
he loud, the troublemakers, the
rule breakers, the rule followers
e enthusiasts, the skeptics, the
ounting, Deanna from Human
he fixers, the bold, the timid, the
dent, the under-confident, the
eople people," the hard cases
bies, and the forces for change

*This book is
the start of a movement
to improve 10 million
working relationships*

#BestPossibleRelationship
BestPossibleRelationship.com

Michael Bungay Stanier

How to Work with (ALMOST) Anyone.

Five Questions for Building the
Best Possible Relationships

PAGE TWO

Cataloguing in publication information is
available from Library and Archives Canada.
ISBN 978-1-77458-265-7 (paperback)
ISBN 978-1-77458-266-4 (ebook)

Page Two
pagetwo.com

Edited by Kendra Ward
Copyedited by Jenny Govier
Proofread by Alison Strobel
Cover and interior design by Peter Cocking
Printed and bound in Canada by Friesens
Distributed in Canada by Raincoast Books
Distributed in the US and internationally by Macmillan

23 24 25 26 27   5 4 3 2 1

Visit MBS.works for the confidence, community, and programs to
help you unlock your greatness and the greatness of others.

Visit BoxOfCrayons.com for more information
on training and culture change for organizations.

To all the people I've worked

with over the years.

Thank you for teaching me about what

it means to work well together.

Contents

_____

Love is a verb.

ESTHER PEREL

The Best Possible Relationship

Working relationships that are safe, vital, and repairable

Stop Leaving It to Chance

Your happiness and your success depend on your working relationships. The people you manage. How well you work with your boss. The way collaboration happens with colleagues and peers. How you connect with important prospects and key clients.

But the hard truth is this: most of us leave the health and fate of these relationships to chance. We say "Hi," exchange pleasantries, hope for the best, and immediately get into the work.

No wonder. What needs doing is urgent, demanding, and right there. So, you roll up your sleeves and jump in, all the while crossing your fingers and offering up a prayer to the gods that the other person is as good as they seem... well, is half-decent... actually, you just hope they don't turn out to be a nightmare. (Most of us have been disappointed enough times to have significantly lowered expectations.)

Soon (sometimes it takes weeks, sometimes minutes), the first cracks appear. A misunderstanding. An expectation not met. A low-grade irritation. A random act of weirdness. Different ways of seeing the world or getting things done. A flare-up under stress.

In short, disappointment.

Every relationship becomes suboptimal at some point, whether it's a good one that goes off the rails or one that was poor from the start. When suboptimal happens, most of us don't know what to do about it. We blame them, or ourselves, or the universe (or maybe all three). We get all the feelings: sad, let down, irritated, frustrated. But mostly we are resigned to the fact that this is what happens: relationships always get a little broken, or a little stale, or a little worse. *C'est la vie, c'est la guerre.* Carry on.

But it doesn't have to be like this.

Every Working Relationship Can Be Better

Imagine if you could:

- Keep the brilliant relationships humming for as long as possible.

- Contain the dysfunction of the messy ones so they're less painful and more productive.

- Reset the solidly OK ones so that when they wobble, they more quickly get back on track.

For all of these, an essential part of the solution is the same: actively build the Best Possible Relationship (BPR). When you commit to a BPR, you commit to intentionally designing and managing the way you work with people, rather than just accepting what happens. With a BPR you create relationships that are safe, vital, and repairable. That's the foundation for happier, more successful working partnerships.

The BPR: Safe. Vital. Repairable.

Vitruvian Man is one of Leonardo da Vinci's iconic drawings: a naked man faces us, arms and legs in two different positions, within both a circle and a square. It's

Create relationships that are safe, vital, and repairable.

---

meant to show ideal human proportions and is named for the Roman architect Vitruvius, who proposed that the three essential attributes of a building were *firmitas* (strength), *utilitas* (utility), and *venustas* (beauty).

We're not erecting a temple to Diana here, but we do need our own principles to understand the foundation of a Best Possible Relationship. "Strength, utility, and beauty" are pretty good options, but we can do better.

Safe is about removing fear. Harvard Business School's Amy Edmondson, a champion for the idea of psychological safety, codified it as this:

A belief that one will not be punished or humiliated for speaking up with ideas, questions, concerns, or mistakes, and that the team is safe for interpersonal risk-taking.

A robust body of research confirms that psychological safety creates individual and team success by unlocking the benefits of diversity, increasing agility with change, and expanding the capacity to innovate.

Not only do the risks of *speaking up* make people feel "less than" at work. Too many fear even *showing up*. A study from Deloitte in 2013 talked about "covering," a sociological term for the way people with stigmatized identities downplayed that identity, hiding it as much as possible. The study found that almost two-thirds of employees play down parts of their identity. The Google research initiative on management, Project Oxygen, recently added the ability to "create an inclusive team environment, showing concern for success and well-being" as a necessary characteristic of a great manager.

Vital is about amplifying the good. I've chosen the word for its dual meanings: both essential *and* enlivening. Vital acknowledges "safe" as table stakes, and then asks: What's the game, and what are we playing for? It encapsulates the Dan Pink trinity from *Drive*: people's motivation comes from a sense of purpose, autonomy, and mastery. Vital means constructing a working relationship with the right combination of support and challenge, one where you each have the best chance to do work that matters, take responsibility for and make your own choices, and learn and grow.

Repairable speaks to the reality that all relationships have some degree of fragility and will have moments of being both cracked (damaged from within) and dented (damaged from without). "Safe" and "vital" are all well and good, but if they crumble at the slightest injury, then the relationship lacks resilience. "Best possible relationship" doesn't mean there are never difficult moments, but rather there's commitment and capacity to fix the damage and carry on. This stops harm from escalating and ossifying and allows a relationship to reset and, often, to continue more strongly than before.

The impacts of safe, vital, and repairable relationships are felt at the individual and organizational levels. Better work being done. Better retention of essential people. Better mental health. More flourishing and engagement. And fewer required HR interventions, from arbitrating through to firing.

The Keystone Conversation

At the heart of creating a Best Possible Relationship lies the **Keystone Conversation**. In architecture, a keystone sits at the top of the arch, bridging the two sides, locking them together in stable equilibrium, and allowing the arch to bear weight. As the keystone settles over time, the arch becomes more stable. Without a keystone, the arch collapses.

People join
an organization but
leave a manager.
You don't want to *be*
that manager.
You don't want to
have that manager.

———————————

In 1969, zoologist Robert Paine adapted the idea. Now, in biology the keystone species is one that disproportionately affects its environment relative to the species' abundance. It is the organizing force for a healthy ecology; without it, the ecosystem would be radically different or collapse altogether.

When grey wolves were reintroduced into Yellowstone National Park in 1995 after a seventy-year absence, a cascade of changes began that continue today. More wolves meant less time for elk to forage, and so more robust and diverse vegetation proliferated, including willows. More willows meant more songbirds and more beavers. More beavers changed the shape of the river. The changed river meant an increase in fish. And so it goes, more resilient and more diverse, evolving and flourishing.

You can pick your preferred metaphor, architecture or ecology. In either case, the keystone allows the system to bear stress, stay healthy, and grow stronger over time. We're striving for the same outcomes with the Keystone Conversation.

Here's how you use the Keystone Conversation to start building a Best Possible Relationship. First, **prepare** by asking yourself the **five essential questions:**

The Amplify Question: What's your best?

The Steady Question: What are your practices and preferences?

The Good Date Question: What can you learn from successful past relationships?

The Bad Date Question: What can you learn from frustrating past relationships?

The Repair Question: How will you fix it when things go wrong?

The questions are straightforward and powerful. They're easy enough to answer quickly… and they take some work to answer well. Their magic is that they create a conversation that is atypical in most working relationships. In the pages that follow, there are prompts and space for you to answer each of the five questions. You'll be surprised by what you discover about yourself.

Then, you need to **have the conversation**. It will feel awkward at first, but there are ways of doing it with more ease and less stress, both for you and for the other person. I'll share strategies about how you invite someone to have this conversation, then how you make it less tricky and weird at the start, more useful in the middle, and what it takes to end strongly.

Finally, you need to keep your BPR alive and thriving by applying regular **maintenance**, so that it stays safe, vital, and repairable. Like almost anything we create, the relationship needs to be cared for.

There's a bonus section, Know Your Stuff. "Know thyself," said the ancients, and that's a helpful directive for the Keystone Conversation and any BPR. This section includes exercises to help you be more articulate and insightful about who you are, both the shadow and the light.

But What's Success?
(It's Not What You'd Expect)

The Keystone Conversation builds the infrastructure for a Best Possible Relationship by establishing three things.

First, it generates a **shared responsibility**. Creating a BPR is an unexpected and often countercultural act in many organizations. Caring for this relationship that's so central to success and happiness is both people's responsibility. How will *we*, together and individually, work towards this shared objective?

Second, the Keystone Conversation creates **permission** to continue to talk about the relationship in the good times and (crucially) the hard times ahead. It acknowledges that things won't always be great and the relationship will need to be adjusted and repaired, reset, and revitalized. Once you've started asking each other, "How do we want this to be?" you can then ask, "How are we doing?" The shared goal of a Best Possible Relationship becomes a permitted (and, ideally, normalized) topic of conversation.

Finally, and most obviously, the Keystone Conversation gives you a **deeper understanding** of the person across the table from you. You might have felt at times that others don't fully appreciate all that you are, your complexity and nuances. The person across the table feels *exactly* the same. Creating incomplete and inaccurate stories about who the other person is, what animates them, and what they can give is so easy. This conversation brings you closer to the truth of the story and of the humanity of the other person.

Not Therapy, Not Tinder.
But Maybe . . . Radical

This is a short book that's full of practical value. It's not a deep psychological dive (although it draws on that wisdom), nor does it offer easy "swipe right" hacks. Rather, it's in the sweet spot to help you improve your important working relationships using practical, everyday tools.

It will be helpful if you work with other human beings, no matter if you're at the start of your career or well established in it, whether you're a manager or an individual contributor. It works for relationships within your organization and with stakeholders beyond it. You can use the tools no matter if you're trying to start things off on the right foot or looking to improve a working relationship that's already underway.

But know this: in its application, this work is also radical.

When I showed an early version of this book to a friend of mine, a senior exec at a well-known Silicon Valley company, she suggested I acknowledge how much bravery and energy it takes to invest in a BPR. This is, she said, not a normal way of working in most organizations. She's right. And if you've been reading this so far with a hint of skepticism about whether this is possible, you're not alone. It's a common first reaction.

When you take on building Best Possible Relationships and having Keystone Conversations, you'll meet resistance, not least your own. You will likely be disrupting current expectations of how hierarchy, power, and leadership can work. It will be unusual, awkward, and unexpected—and that's if you do it with people you manage. If you do this with other relationships beyond your direct reports, it's even less expected. It *does* get easier, but like any new skill it will be hard at first. You'll be creating a new way of working with people.

The author William Gibson said that "the future is already here—it's just not very evenly distributed." When you adopt these methods, you're choosing to be the future. It's all well and good to talk about creating psychological safety and a workplace in which people flourish. This is one of the ways you do it.

Hard-Won Wisdom

In my thirty or so years of starting, being thrown into, growing, breaking, nurturing, ignoring, repairing, betraying, celebrating, and ending working relationships, I've been loved, and I've been thoroughly disliked. Some people have brought out the best in me, while some have managed (temporarily, thank goodness) to crush my spirit, soul, resolve, and confidence. I've also done those things to others.

These successes and failures of mine are hard-won wisdom, and I've put what I've learned and what works in this book. If you'd like to build the Best Possible Relationships with your key people, read on.

Who's Your BPR Person?

It's helpful to have a person in mind as you work through the book. Do so, and you'll be better able to imagine how the Keystone Conversation will work in your life. On the next page I've included a "build your own" menu of sorts, so you can identify some of the characteristics that might nudge you towards one person or another who'd be useful as someone with whom you might like to build a BPR.

Identify Your BPR Person

RELATIONSHIP

- ☐ A direct report
- ☐ Your boss
- ☐ A peer
- ☐ A key colleague
- ☐ A senior player
- ☐ Someone with influence
- ☐ Someone with resources
- ☐ A gatekeeper
- ☐ A vendor
- ☐ A prospect
- ☐ A client

RELATIONSHIP STAGE

- ☐ Onboarding
- ☐ Brand new
- ☐ Early days
- ☐ In the middle of the journey
- ☐ Coming to its end

RELATIONSHIP HEALTH

- ☐ Untested
- ☐ A thing of beauty
- ☐ Frustrating and broken
- ☐ Perfectly adequate
- ☐ Going stale

WHY DOES IT MATTER TO YOU?

☐ I'm committed to having my people flourish

☐ I want to set us up for success

☐ How we're currently working together is a source of unhappiness

☐ I want to keep a good thing going

☐ I feel like we've accepted mediocrity

☐ I want a relationship of trust and accountability

☐ How we're currently working together is a source of anger and frustration

☐ I want to lessen future disappointments

☐ I want to be braver/clearer/more transparent in how I show up in working relationships

☐ If we don't course correct now, it might be too late

So... who's your person?

Download a template to help you identify your BPR person (and get other resources) at BestPossibleRelationship.com, or follow the QR code.

And so each venture

is a new beginning,

a raid on the inarticulate

T.S. ELIOT

The Five Questions of the Keystone Conversation

What you need to talk about when you talk about working together

Preparing
for the
Keystone
Conversation

To fund my university days I worked as a dishwasher, so I thought I knew what went on in restaurants. But only when I started watching shows like *Chef's Table* did I come to appreciate how much work goes into a great meal.

I understood that the chef decided what to offer on the menu. I'd also seen the drama of the cooking itself: orders being shouted, lots of people stirring and grilling, saucing, and plating, with everyone yelling "Yes, chef!" all the time. But I didn't realize that the kitchen started hours before with a relentless amount of preparation. Slicing and trimming vegetables so they were the perfect shape, readying the cuts of various proteins, making the sauces. You can only cook a fantastic meal when you've got the ingredients you need on hand.

The coming pages provide the moment to metaphorically put on your apron and sharpen your knives as you prepare for a Keystone Conversation. In them you'll find the five questions that shape a Keystone Conversation, a Core Exercise to help prompt your thinking, and the space to articulate your answers. Some answers will be straightforward, others less so. Here's what's ahead.

The Amplify Question—What's your best?—helps you name your most important qualities. It stands alongside such disciplines as positive psychology, Appreciative Inquiry, and the positive deviance approach to change, where the clarion call is to focus on what's working. Call it "turn it up to 11" (*Spinal Tap*) or "more cowbell" (*SNL*), but it's all about amplifying the good.

The Steady Question—What are your practices and preferences?—acknowledges that we're all creatures of habit. There's a steady predictability to much of what you do and how. The more you can explain to others the details of how you like to work, the easier it is for them to support your best. This question can be illuminating because habits are, by definition, unconscious actions. It often helps you recognize your preferred ways of working for the first time.

The Good Date and Bad Date Questions—What can you learn from successful/frustrating past relationships?— recognize that although all your past relationships had their individual quirks, they provide good data about patterns of success and failure. By drawing on lessons of the past, you'll be able to double down on what works and avoid what doesn't. Your answers here will help you actively construct an environment where you're most likely to flourish.

Finally, **the Repair Question**—How will you fix it when things go wrong?—leans into the uncomfortable truth that every working relationship will have its rough patches. This question doesn't believe that "time heals all wounds." Nor does it assume that once things break they must stay broken. Rather, it opens up the ways you might accelerate getting back on track after disappointments, disruptions, and moments of being stuck.

Step Back, Gordon

Good news: preparing your answers to the five questions isn't as intense as being in a kitchen with Gordon Ramsay yelling, "It's f*@cking raw!" as you do the work. Take your time. Be brave, be vulnerable, be truthful.

Don't be modest about what's good, and don't skip over the messier parts of who you are. You don't have to share every insight you uncover, but the more robust your preparation is, the more material you'll have to draw from to shape your BPR.

GO A LITTLE DEEPER?

It's absolutely fine to answer the five questions with the level of self-awareness you have now and whatever the Core Exercises bring to light. But if you're interested in expanding your understanding, the bonus Know Your Stuff section towards the end of the book offers some deep-dive exercises that might intrigue you and prove helpful.

Download a template to help you answer the five questions and prepare for the Keystone Conversation (and get other resources) at BestPossibleRelationship.com, or follow the QR code.

The Amplify Question: What's Your Best?

Free Solo documents Alex Honnold successfully climbing El Capitan in Yosemite National Park. El Capitan is a granite wall that goes up and up and up, more than 3,000 feet/900 metres from bottom to top. It takes most teams two or three days to climb it using ropes, carabiners, and those tents you can hang off the side of a mountain. Honnold climbed it by himself and without ropes—"free solo"—in a smidge under four hours. It's hard to keep breathing as you watch him ascend.

Don't think for a moment that Honnold just showed up one day and scampered up the wall. Part of the power of the documentary is showing his multi-year obsession: training, choreographing, visualizing, and endlessly, relentlessly practising. When he climbed, Honnold knew precisely how he needed to shift through space and where every single hand- and foothold was going to be.

It was similar for the most famous climb of all: the first ascent of Mount Everest in 1953. Over six weeks Edmund Hillary and Tenzing Norgay went back and forth and up and down more than forty times, establishing camps, exploring what was ahead, formalizing routes, and acclimatizing, practising, until finally on May 29 they summited.

Both are stories of people who, literally, had a peak moment. These moments of being at their best intertwine three elements. First, their natural talents: power and grace, muscle and lung. Then there's the way those strengths are focused and honed over time, how a thousand small failures have shown the path to success, and how practice and experience have created mastery. Finally, there's finding the right moment and context to fully express what's taken a lifetime so far to learn.

Summiting

Not many of us seek high-mountain glory. But we've all had the chance to discover our talents, work towards mastery, and understand the situations where and when we're at our best. That's why the first question of the

Keystone Conversation is: **What's your best?** It asks you to name what creates your peak moments, your talents, what you love to do and are good at, and when you tend to shine.

The Power of the Amplify Question

A fundamental choice when you're wrestling with change at an individual or organizational level is this: Do you focus on what's not working, or on what is? The general bias is towards fixing. But there's a subset of change experts who think amplifying what's already working is the best primary strategy. How do you take what's good and make it louder, brighter, better? How do you build pathways rather than fill potholes?

Your strengths can encompass technical, emotional, and relational talents. But being good at something doesn't automatically make it a strength. Marcus Buckingham, author of various books on the subject, says, "A strength is an activity that strengthens you. It draws you in, it makes time fly by while you're doing it, and it makes you feel strong." You can be good at something and still find it drains you rather than boosts you.

The curse of competence traps you doing what you're good at but not fulfilled by.

———————————

You will be happier and more successful if you use your strengths more of the time. When you and another person tell each other what your strengths are, you gain information about how your BPR can bring them out in both of you.

CORE EXERCISE
Good At versus Fulfilled By

The answer to "What's your best?" isn't just about identifying what you are good at. In fact, you could become manacled by what you are half-decent at, because collapsing "good at" into "fulfilled by" is annoyingly easy. When you are good at something you don't enjoy, you become trapped by your own skill level. You do it well, so people give it to you to do. You do it well, so you think it's yours to do. You do it well, so you don't wholly trust others to do it. That's the curse of competence.

A powerful outcome of this exercise is to be able to say in the Keystone Conversation: "I'm good at this… and I don't love doing it."

To do this exercise, you tease apart "good at" and "fulfilled by." Work with a two-by-two matrix—a box with a cross separating it into four equal spaces. One axis is I'm Good At (low to high), the other I'm Fulfilled By (also low to high). Consider your key responsibilities and most common day-to-day tasks and assign them to the appropriate box.

If you're lucky, you'll have several tasks in the High/ High box: you're both good at and fulfilled by them. If you're hungry to learn and grow, you'll be delighted to see a few things in the Low Good At/High Fulfilled By box. And if you're human, you'll have items in the diagonally opposite box: Low Fulfilled By, High Good At.

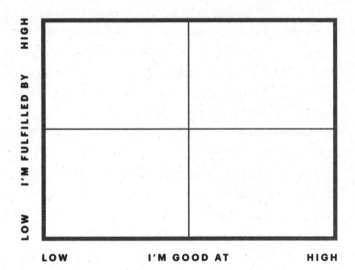

How would you answer the Amplify Question:

WHAT'S YOUR BEST?

_____

_____

_____

_____

_____

_____

_____

_____

GO A LITTLE DEEPER?

Deepen your answers with these two exercises in Know Your Stuff (p. 171):

Archetypes • The Boasting Friend

Download a template to help you answer the five questions and prepare for the Keystone Conversation (and get other resources) at BestPossibleRelationship.com, or follow the QR code.

The Steady Question: What Are Your Practices and Preferences?

When I'm interviewed on a podcast, I'm occasion-
ally asked to name a favourite book. My go-to is
Bill Bryson's *A Short History of Nearly Everything*.
If you found that high school sucked all joy out of
science, this book will breathe back life. Bryson doesn't
just make the science fascinating. He makes the world
we live in feel more magical and more extraordinary.

An early chapter explains how much had to occur
for our twenty-first-century life to happen, and he points
to our moon as an example. We have a ridiculously large
moon relative to the size of our planet. As a compar-
ison, check out the sizes of Io, Europa, Ganymede, and
the other seventy-some satellites of Jupiter. They're
teeny-weeny.

"So what?" you might ask.

The size of our moon keeps the Earth from wobbling
too erratically on its axis. That creates consistent and
predictable seasons. Which means not only can we

schedule a good summer vacation, but more importantly we can cultivate the land and grow food. Wheat when it's spring. Summer strawberries. Apples in the autumn.

A consistent cycle of crops allowed civilization to begin and flourish. Over 50 percent of humanity now lives in cities, and our progress (with the light and the dark that this encompasses) is rooted in our rootedness. In other words, there might be life on Earth, but you wouldn't be reading this book now if it wasn't for the Moon's solid work over the last several billion years in stabilizing the planet.

A Steady Axis

You too have a steady axis and keep a steady beat. Oh, don't get me wrong: parts of you are erratic and random. But there are ways in which you are thoroughly predictable and solidly consistent. You travel your own ruts and grooves.

The second question of the Keystone Conversation asks you to make those ways explicit: **What are your practices and preferences?**

The Power of the Steady Question

Over time, you've developed and refined how you work. Some practices you're aware of. They're common sense to you but possibly quirky and perhaps even inexplicable to others. There are other practices that you're blind to because they're unconscious and you've never been asked to name them.

A BPR can't necessarily accommodate every one of your preferred ways of interacting. But knowing your preferences and sharing them means that, together, you'll be able to look at where your practices are the same and where they're different and might cause conflict. You'll also see how, between the two of you, you can accommodate the different ways in which you like to work.

CORE EXERCISE
Deep Read Me

A popular approach to building working relationships with others is the "Read Me" document. The idea is that you fill out your Ways of Doing Things and then send it out to people. "If I were an IKEA bookshelf," the promise is, "then this is how you'd assemble me for minimum wobble and maximum Nordic aesthetic."

It's a great start. Tell people whether you're a morning person or an evening person, when you do and don't respond to communication, whether you prefer Slack or email, how you like feedback delivered, and so on.

But know the limitations of the Read Me's. First, they're all very me-me-me. "I like this, and I want that, and I expect the other." Second, they assume that by loftily informing others of your patterns and preferences, you've completed the work. That's unlikely. The few people who read those documents rarely remember much of them. That's why we're using the structure of the Read Me to prepare for a conversational exchange.

For this exercise, list your preferences. Here are nine things particularly helpful to be clear on:

- What's your name? What's not your name? What other language around identity, if any, is important to you?

- Are you an extrovert or an introvert? What does that mean to you, and how does that show up in how you work?

- What time of day do you work best?

- What communication quirks do you have? Channel preferences? Abbreviations? Patterns of responding or not responding?

- What does a good meeting look like to you? What's not a good meeting?

- What feedback tends to be most helpful to you? How do you prefer it to be expressed?

- How do you manage deadlines and milestones? Do you work consistently, or does it tend to happen in a rush at the end?

- Do you start with the big picture and work towards the details, or vice versa?

- What seemingly small thing drives you nuts?

How would you answer the Steady Question:
WHAT ARE YOUR PRACTICES AND PREFERENCES?

_____

_____

_____

_____

_____

GO A LITTLE DEEPER?

Deepen your answers with these two exercises in Know Your Stuff (p. 177):
Where Did You Learn Your Work Habits? •
Calm or Volatile?

Download a template to help you answer the five questions and prepare for the Keystone Conversation (and get other resources) at BestPossibleRelationship.com, or follow the QR code.

The Good Date Question: What Can You Learn from Successful Past Relationships?

As a very minor player in the world of "content creation," I've had to learn the ropes of shooting video in a studio. I was lucky that one of my earliest collaborators and mentors, Mark Bowden, has been a director and film actor: all the close-ups of the Orc General in *The Lord of the Rings* movies are of Mark wearing a *lot* of makeup.

Each of the thirty or so videos in the training program that Mark and I created together had its own setup. When you make a design decision like that, you realize why there are so many people in a film crew. There's a lot of stuff to arrange, rearrange, re-rearrange... and then fine-tune.

Trickiest of all seems to be lighting. Many of us had a pandemic-inspired crash course on How to Look Less Corpse-Like on Zoom. But filming with three or four cameras is a whole other level. The main light, the spotlight, the back light, shadows where you need them and light where you don't. People are forever tinkering, moving stuff a little to the left or the right, turning the brightness up and down, adding and removing filters.

Shine

But when you're with a lighting maestro, the result is magic. Wherever "the talent" stands, they're illuminated to look their best. They shine. You've had your moments too when you've glowed in a working relationship. You can't put that down to a good ring light, a layer of foundation, and some deftly applied hair gel. That's why the third question of the Keystone Conversation encourages you to share the story and the insights from what's worked before: **What can you learn from successful past relationships?**

The Power of the Good Date Question

Bring to mind one of your favourite past working relationships—a boss or a direct report or a peer or a vendor or someone with whom the experience was noticeably better than the others. You felt seen and understood; you found the right balance between challenge and support. You found connection and alignment, and good work got done. They brought out your best, and you did the same for them.

It felt ridiculously easy, actually. You "clicked," and things went well. When there was a hiccup, it didn't seem to matter that much: you figured it out between you. If anything, managing that stress strengthened the relationship rather than damaging it.

It was probably part luck, part timing, and part hard work on both sides of the equation. But somehow, between the two of you, you got the lighting right. There's wisdom to be gleaned from this success. Mine it for all it's worth. Figure out how you made it happen.

CORE EXERCISE
How Did You Build It?

We're typically rubbish at accurately assigning responsibility for success. The so-called self-serving cognitive bias means we give more weight than is due to our own role in what works; we also place more blame on the other person for what isn't working.

So, start this exercise by celebrating the other person's role in the success of the relationship.

- What did they say (and also not say)? What words made a difference?

- What did they do (and also not do)? What actions elevated and nurtured the relationship?

- How did they "be"? What qualities did they exhibit that added to the goodness of what was there?

Now that you've given them due credit, take the credit that's yours to claim. Don't be overly modest here. The relationship was so good in part because of the way you showed up.

- What did you say (and also not say)? What were your well-measured words?

- What did you do (and also not do)? What big and small actions added to the good?

- How did you "be"? How did you show up in a way that helped you both put your best foot forward?

We often underestimate the setting of success. It happens not just because of you and them. The time

and place contributed to things working well. What
do you notice about that?

- What about the context gave this relationship the
  best chance to flourish? Who else played a role?
- Which moment tested the relationship, a test
  that you successfully managed? What light does
  that shed?

**How would you answer the Good Date Question: WHAT
CAN YOU LEARN FROM SUCCESSFUL PAST RELATIONSHIPS?**

GO A LITTLE DEEPER?

Deepen your answers with these two exercises in Know Your Stuff (p. 183):
How Did They Love You? • *Hide & Seek*

 Download a template to help you answer the five questions and prepare for the Keystone Conversation (and get other resources) at BestPossibleRelationship.com, or follow the QR code.

The Bad Date Question: What Can You Learn from Frustrating Past Relationships?

Netflix's *Stranger Things* didn't just bring the Upside Down and all its attendant horrors. It made Dungeons & Dragons cool for a new generation. I'm of the old generation. I started playing D&D in my teens, and my friends and I would play weekend-long games, with the occasional breaks for backyard cricket.

When a tournament came to town, we entered the competition and we slayed (literally and metaphorically). We were untouchable. Whenever we shot an arrow, it would kill not one orc but three. When we needed to roll a 100—a 1 percent chance—we did that and unlocked the Big Secret that ensured our victory. It. Was. Glorious.

Twelve months later, the tournament came around again. We hadn't played in the ensuing year—pressures of schoolwork, trying to get a date, etc., etc.—but we still had our swagger from the previous year's success.

This was an utterly different experience. Our Dungeon Master was not so easily charmed/bullied as the previous one had been. We started badly (significant damage from an ambush in the first four minutes), staggered around the corner to be wounded by a Gelatinous Cube, and finally expired when the booby-trapped flagstone unleashed a thunderstorm of crossbow bolts. We'd been playing for exactly eighteen minutes, and we were out of the tournament.

It Starts Bad and Goes Downhill

The small mercy was that at least our D&D death was a quick one. The same can't be said of some working relationships. You know how it goes. You arrive hopeful. You're excited to start off down the path together. But for some reason it begins badly and only gets increasingly messy, difficult, confusing, and frustrating as time goes on.

But those past experiences are now a rich source of wisdom. They show you what conditions you need to flourish and (juicier) the ways you behave badly to undermine and sabotage relationships. That's why the fourth question in the Keystone Conversation is the flipside of the third: **What can you learn from frustrating past relationships?**

The Power of the Bad Date Question

Some of the most valuable bits of "intel" you can share
in the Keystone Conversation are details of past working
relationships that have been a struggle. The instinct is
to cover them up or blame the other party for the mess,
but doing so is a mistake. Yes, the other person played
their role. But you were part of the dynamic as well.

The experience likely felt deeply personal and
unique—which it was—but at the same time, it also
expressed a repeating pattern. The details you uncover
will offer clues to recurring dynamics that you might
want to avoid or at least actively manage this time
around. There's "wisdom in the wound." Examine your
behaviour, their behaviour, and the situation, and see
what you can learn from those past difficult experiences.

CORE EXERCISE
How Did You Break It?

This is the alter-ego exercise to How Did
You Build It? in the previous chapter. In that exercise,
I asked first what *they* did and then what *you* did to
counteract the human tendency to take more than

our due credit for the good things. Now, to manage the flipside bias to assign more blame to the others than to yourself when things go bad, let's start with you taking your share of the "credit" for the mess.

- What did you say (and also not say)? What words and silences caused damage?

- What did you do (and also not do)? What small and big actions undermined any good intentions?

- How did you "be"? How did you show up in a way that soured dynamics?

But not only you made it hard. Don't take all the blame. How did the other party contribute to the mess?

- What did they say (and also not say)? What got you angry or frustrated or sad?

- What did they do (and also not do)? What actions set things back?

- How did they "be"? What qualities did they exhibit that, frankly, sucked?

Finally, it wasn't only you and them. The time and place always influence what happens. What do you notice here about the context?

- What about the context made this odds-against? What other people played a role?

- Which moment tested the relationship, a moment you failed to navigate and that was particularly damaging? What light does that shed?

How would you answer the Bad Date Question: WHAT CAN YOU LEARN FROM FRUSTRATING PAST RELATIONSHIPS?

_____

_____

_____

_____

_____

_____

_____

GO A LITTLE DEEPER?

Deepen your answers with these two exercises in Know Your Stuff (p. 189):

What Do People Get Wrong about You? •
Claim Your Villain

 Download a template to help you answer the five questions and prepare for the Keystone Conversation (and get other resources) at BestPossibleRelationship.com, or follow the QR code.

The Repair Question: How Will You Fix It When Things Go Wrong?

One video of the Tōhoku earthquake and tsunami that struck Japan in 2011 is particularly terrible and mesmerizing. I thought a tsunami might be something like Hokusai's famous woodblock print *The Great Wave off Kanagawa*: a single, towering foam-flecked arc. But it's nothing like that. In the video, water seemingly slowly rises between banks. A few cars trundle back and forth on the road next to the harbour walls. After two minutes, a boat—a big boat—is ripped from its moorings and swept away. Suddenly, you have a sense of the force at play. At six minutes, the water explodes over the walls, and destruction is immediate. Cars are crushed, infrastructure is torn apart, buildings are lifted off their foundations.

Japan is on a fault line. The history of tidal waves stretching back for hundreds of years is marked on tsunami stones that can be found up and down the northeastern coast. They register the high points of particularly devastating tsunamis and enshrine generational memory about what's safe and what may not be. In 1933, a tsunami, the second in less than forty years, struck the village of Aneyoshi. The stone there reads, "High dwellings are the peace and harmony of our descendants. Remember the calamity of the great tsunamis. Do not build any homes below this point."

Shelter

A little more peace and harmony would be nice. But calamities will keep happening. Every working relationship will have moments of crisis or struggle. Something will go wrong somewhere. That's completely predictable. But doing something about it is hard. So often we let situations deteriorate. That's why the final question of the Keystone Conversation can be so encouraging and liberating: **How will you fix it when things go wrong?**

The Power of the Repair Question

There's no doubt: this question competes with the "bad relationship" one for most awkward and least easy to answer. What might be helpful to know is that your answers are only the second most important thing. The most important is a shared recognition that things will break. Preparing to answer this question in the Keystone Conversation is a rehearsal for speaking up when things are a little off, or when you've been let down, or when you've done damage.

There is a risk that the other person will not see what's broken. We all fear a "Huh, what are you talking about?" response. Mr. Rogers said, "Anything that's human is mentionable, and anything that is mentionable can be more manageable." By understanding that it will break and talking about it before it does, you'll be better able to notice when it's failing and repair it together.

CORE EXERCISE
Bridging

When the European Union first formed in the early 1990s, there were far fewer member states than there are now. One of the many challenges faced by the so called "Inner Six"—Belgium, France, Italy, Luxembourg, the Netherlands, and West Germany—was how to combine their currencies. They needed to determine what the new euro banknotes would look like.

What kind of design would be unifying rather than divisive and collective rather than nationalistic?

The answer was bridges. After a minor hiccup—bridge nerds pointed out that the "imaginary" designs first presented were all pretty much based on real bridges—the final design showed seven styles of bridges from different eras: stone arcs, iron span bridges, cable bridges, and so on.

Work relationships get damaged and we turn away from one another. One way to repair them is by building a bridge back to connection. It takes courage and skill to do this. It often requires a generosity, a softening of your stance, and a commitment to a bigger game to be the person who begins the repair.

In this exercise, think back to relationships you've made better. What strategies did you use? These might be deployed in the so-called heat of the battle, and they might also be used in the aftermath.

I know these don't always feel available. After all, even conflict mediators get into arguments. However, at your best, which ones do you tend to draw upon? Can you do the following?

- **Name what's happening:** Surface the unspoken; name what's going on for you.

- **Stay curious:** Breathe rather than react; stay open; examine your defensiveness and your righteousness; remember they're human too.

- **Remember the goal:** Understand what "winning" means; hold on to the idea of the Best Possible Relationship; let go of "being right."

- **Seek understanding:** Listen fully so they feel heard; tease apart fact and data from opinion and judgment.

- **De-escalate:** Introduce lightness and grace; own your statements (less "you did ..." and more "I make up that ..."); turn down the heat.

- **Rebuild:** Make the first move to reconnect; reframe it away from "you versus me"; apologize.

Identifying and sharing strategies you use to build bridges helps people understand when bridges are being built.

How would you answer the Repair Question:

HOW WILL YOU FIX IT WHEN THINGS GO WRONG?

_____

_____

_____

_____

_____

_____

_____

GO A LITTLE DEEPER?

Deepen your answers with these two exercises in Know Your Stuff (p. 197):

Is That a Cigar? • *Stressed Out*

 Download a template to help you answer the five questions and prepare for the Keystone Conversation (and get other resources) at BestPossibleRelationship.com, or follow the QR code.

Hey—
it's Michael here,
the author.

Yes, that's my blood, sweat, and tears that
you're seeing blotting the text…

If you're enjoying the read, would you consider
giving the book a review on your preferred
online retailer's website or reading community?
This "social proof" that this book is worth
it really helps it succeed in the world. And if
you're not so moved, no worries at all.

BestPossibleRelationship.com
#BestPossibleRelationship

Utterance is magic.

Words do have power. Names have power. Words are events, they do things, change things. They transform both speaker and hearer.

URSULA K. LE GUIN

How to Have a Keystone Conversation

Start safe, ensure
it's useful in the middle,
and finish strong

Running the Keystone Conversation

The first Keystone Conversation I had, before I had any idea what I was doing or why, was on a bus. I was sitting next to the woman whom I'd eventually marry, and we were heading for Stratford-upon-Avon to see something by Shakespeare. Ominously enough it was *The Winter's Tale*. That's the play where one of the characters exits pursued by a bear: not exactly a role model for happy relationship endings.

We were a couple of weeks into a relationship that we were both extremely surprised to find ourselves in. We'd each arrived in England to do graduate study, with no intention of getting into a relationship anytime soon. But somehow, here we were, winding our way through narrow streets and getting serious. We discussed our expectations about children, fidelity, money, and a bunch of other "yes or no" topics. I don't think I brought up, "I'll be featuring you in all my books" (it would probably have been a deal breaker), but we seemed to cover all the other important things. It was the moment when everything changed.

The Keystone Conversation is where the BPR begins to be built.

A Plan

This next section lays out a structure of a Keystone Conversation. My wife and I got lucky: trapped on a back seat together, we found the space to have this discussion. But most of the time, this won't happen unless you take a big breath and make it happen.

The unknown-ness of it could paralyze you. "How do I make the invite? How do I start? What's the middle like? How do we finish?" All of that's covered in the coming pages. You'll notice a slight shift in tone. You don't need paragraphs at this stage, you need an instruction manual and scripts. That's why, ahead, there are two main subheadings: "Do This" and "Say This." Of course, when I write, "Do This," I mean find your own way to put this into action. And "Say This" means use the words exactly as they're written or create your own variations. The prompts are meant to make it easier to start. You can choose the ones that feel most natural and tweak them however you like.

This won't happen unless you take a big breath and make it happen.

You might be thinking, "Won't this Keystone Conversation be weird/awkward/difficult?" The answer is: Yes. Certainly, the first few times you have one, it will feel uncomfortable, unusual, and vulnerable. This book is meant as a step towards "unweirding" the conversation.

More to the point, feeling awkward during a Keystone Conversation is normal, not some failure of you or of them or of the process. You're co-creating something important and rare, a Best Possible Relationship. You're figuring out a new way of working together and shaping a different future. You're shifting the foundations of success. It would be surprising if it weren't a little complex and challenging.

But you're still reading, so I'm guessing you understand the power and the importance of this ... and I sense you're up for the adventure.

Read on.

 See me role-model a Keystone Conversation at BestPossibleRelationship.com, or follow the QR code.

Invitation:
Make the
First Move

I remember my first school dance. It was like that scene from *Harry Potter and the Goblet of Fire*, where everyone is learning to waltz in preparation for the Yule Ball. The boys sweating it out on one side of the room. The girls rolling their eyes on the other.

There were fewer magic wands at Torrens Primary School in the 1970s, but other than that things were Exactly. The. Same. I really, really, *really* didn't want to walk across the room and ask Pauline Wade to dance. But someone has to make the first move, and the Keystone Conversation is a dance most people won't be familiar with. If you're hoping they'll initiate it, you'll probably be disappointed.

Be the person who starts.

DO THIS

1. Invite Them to a Keystone Conversation

One of the great freedoms in knowing that this conversation will be awkward at first, and that there will never naturally be a "good time" to have it, is that it leads you logically to deduce that there's never (well, hardly ever) a bad time either. Wherever you are in the arc of a working relationship, consider pausing the current action and inviting that other person to a Keystone Conversation.

You can request this before you first meet. That's a good move when you're starting a long-term working relationship that's going to matter. This could be with someone on a team you are part of or an important client.

You can suggest this in a working relationship that's already begun and is going well. You can propose it in a working relationship that's gone a little stale, one you'd like to reset. You can request it in a relationship that feels stuck and broken.

However, it probably doesn't work to suggest a Keystone Conversation in moments of what author

Amanda Ripley calls "high conflict." Then, the more immediate work is to de-escalate the crisis, repair what's been broken, seek additional support if necessary, and get things back on track. But it's a great idea to broach having one sometime soon after you've fixed what was broken, as a way of disrupting a pattern that might otherwise repeat.

2. Tell Them What the Conversation Is About

Have you ever received an email from your boss that's spiked your anxiety level, a message with some variation on "Please come and see me, I've got some feedback for you"? Don't be that person who invites someone to a Mysterious Meeting That Sounds Like Trouble.

Explain what the Keystone Conversation is, either in person or in writing, and that the point is to give you both the best chance of a successful working relationship.

Share how you'll prepare for the conversation. Give them the five questions. Tell them that you're going to spend some time preparing for the conversation, and recommend that they do the same. Send them a copy of this book or of some of the critical pages. Send them the video of me role-modelling a Keystone Conversation.

Invite them to decide some of the details, such as when and where the conversation will take place.

SAY THIS
Your Word & Phrase Toolkit

These are just prompts. Choose what feels most natural and helpful to you, and tweak however you like.

- I'd like us to chat about how we work together.

- I'd love to spend time figuring out with you what will make this the best possible relationship.

- Could we have a Keystone Conversation where we'll talk about *how* to work together, rather than focusing on *what* to work on? It will give us the best chance to figure out what works, to avoid what doesn't, and to fix the things that get broken.

- Let's chat about how we work together before we talk about what we're working on.

- Before we jump back into what needs to be done/ the project/our priorities, let's talk about how we're working together.

- I want to talk about how we bring out the best in both of us, what things we want to avoid, and how we'll keep this relationship at its best even when the work is hard.

- Here are the five main questions I'd like us to talk about. I've been thinking about my answers, and I want to make sure we both get a chance to ask and answer these:
  1 What's your best?
  2 What are your practices and preferences?
  3 What can we learn from successful past relationships?
  4 What can we learn from frustrating past relationships?
  5 How will we fix it when things go wrong?

 See me role-model a Keystone Conversation at BestPossibleRelationship.com, or follow the QR code.

At the Start: Make It Safe

Humans are newbies on this planet. Tortoises have been nudging along for about 200 million years. Platypuses, 110 million years. Sandhill cranes, 10 million years. We think we're amazing because we've been being human for... well, it depends on who you ask, but let's say half a million years or so, and less than half of that for what the experts call "behavioural modernity."

One thing that's kept us alive is an existential question: Is this dangerous? We have the DNA of our ancestors who erred towards playing it safe. The people who went into the shadowy cave? They didn't survive long enough to become our ancestors.

In *The Coaching Habit* I introduced TERA, my model explaining the neuroscience of engagement. Four drivers make the brain feel safe: Tribe ("Are you with me, or are you against me?"), Expectation ("Do I know the future or don't I?"), Rank ("Are you more important or less important than I am?"), and Autonomy ("Do I get a say or don't I?"). The more you increase the TERA Quotient of any experience, the safer the person will feel, and the more engaged they'll be.

At an unconscious level, the brain uses the TERA criteria five times a second to scan the environment and answer that question: Is it safe, is it safe, is it safe, is it safe, is it safe?

The Keystone Conversation, because it's unusual, feels radical, and because it invites vulnerability, will feel dangerous to everyone's "lizard brain," that most primitive part of the brain that manages fight, flight, or fix. So do all you can to make it unweird and keep it safe.

DO THIS
1. Increase the TERA Quotient

Actively manage the Tribe-iness, clarity of Expectation, Rank, and sense of Autonomy during the Keystone Conversation, so you're keeping the TERA Quotient as high as possible. Here are some of the foundational ways to do that:

- The location of the conversation (whether it's formal or informal; whether it's in "your" space or theirs or somewhere neutral)

- How curious you are (asking questions; asking, "And what else?" after their first answers)

- Your own level of sharing and vulnerability (my rule of thumb is that you answer every question you ask of the other person, sharing the messy and hard, not just the shiny and good)

- The extent to which you co-create the conversation with the other person (asking them what they'd like to ask about; checking if there's anything that needs to be said that hasn't yet been said)

Back in the Invitation stage, you will immediately increase the TERA Quotient by setting a shared goal of a Best Possible Relationship (Tribe); telling them what you'd like to cover (Expectation); reassuring them that you'll share what's going on for you too (Rank); and giving them the choice of when and where they'd like to have the conversation (Autonomy).

2. Be the Strongest Signal in the Room

Because of mirror neurons in our brains, we are constantly and instantly influenced by those with whom we interact. Our moods are catching: whether we feel and embody joy, confidence, or anxiety, they'll likely feel it too.

My friend Mark "The Orc General" Bowden—you'll remember him from before—taught me the power of being "the strongest signal in the room" as a way of shaping any experience. Gandhi, at least according to Instagram wisdom, said, "Be the change you want to see." Take the lead to establish the emotional experience of the Keystone Conversation. One part of your brain will be nudging you to default to anxiety, elusiveness, and defensiveness. That's natural, and you can manage against it. What "mood" do you want to infuse this exchange? I always strive for generous, curious, vulnerable, and delighted, but you will have your own ambitions.

Because my body leads my brain, I've learned how to "hold my body" so that it signals to me (and the other person) the states of being I'm striving for. I deliberately smile, nod my head, laugh when I can, keep my feet on the floor, and keep my hands open. I keep breathing and being curious.

SAY THIS
Your Word & Phrase Toolkit

These are just prompts. Choose what feels most natural and helpful to you, and tweak however you like.

- Thanks for having this conversation with me— it means a lot. (Tribe.)

- What do you want from this conversation? What would make it most helpful for you? Here's what I want. (Tribe. Autonomy.)

- I want to talk about five things: what we are individually best at, our normal patterns of work, what makes for a great working relationship, what happens when things go bad, and how we will fix things when needed. (You'll have communicated this with them at the Invitation stage, but now you're clarifying the agenda.) (Expectation.)

- Where do you want to start? (Rank. Autonomy.)

- Here's the first question I'd like us to answer. (Tribe. Expectation.)

- Do you want to answer this first, or shall I? (Rank. Autonomy.)

- What's been helpful so far? (Rank. Autonomy.)

- Right, mm-hmm, nice, uh-huh, OK, good, sure, yep, lovely. (These small words of encouragement seem meaningless, but they infuse the conversation with encouragement, curiosity, and connection.) (Tribe.)

 Access videos for a deeper dive on TERA at BestPossibleRelationship.com, or follow the QR code.

In the Middle: Ask and Answer

Since the beginning of the COVID pandemic, I've been experimenting with hosting different-from-usual conversations. I started out online. Five people, me included, would Zoom in for an hour. After a short introduction, we'd get to the heart of it: each of us answering a single, provocative question. I'd have sent the question the day before, and it would be chosen to encourage revelation. "What crossroad are you at?" "What lesson do you keep having to learn?" "What needs to be sacrificed so you can go on?" Juicy.

More recently, I've been having these conversations over dinner. In this version, it's me and two others. We introduce ourselves by sharing two essential things about ourselves, and then we each pick one question from a list of five, questions similar to the ones above.

The questions are great, but the real magic is the space people are given to answer the question without needing to solve, decide, fix, or action-item anything. For the online version, the rule was that people had

Nothing needs to be solved, decided, or fixed.

six minutes to speak, and they weren't to be interrupted. More than one person remarked that they couldn't remember a time when they'd spoken for so long and been listened to with such intent.

The Keystone Conversation belongs to the same family as those two formats. Nothing needs to be solved. You're sharing information that's useful, true, and heartfelt. You're listening with intent and seeking to understand.

In *The Coaching Habit*, the mantra is "stay curious a little bit longer, and rush to action and advice-giving a little bit more slowly." The same is true here.

DO THIS
1. Don't Skip the Hard Things

Work through all five questions during the Keystone Conversation. What you don't talk about will become topics that are always hard to talk about. Even asking a single question about a particular topic or giving a short answer will help build your BPR.

It might occur to you to skip the last two questions, because they're about what's not worked or what's not going to work. Why drag skeletons out of the closet? Why imagine the worst? Because if all you do is talk about the good, you'll have neither wisdom nor resilience during the tough times. Most working relationships aren't disastrous, but every working relationship has its share of hurts and misunderstandings and frustrations.

Remember, success is more than answers in the moment. It's also permission to keep talking about how things are going, and the sense that it's safe enough to raise difficult topics. Part of the reason you prepare in advance is so that you know what you want to say. Don't let your nerve fail you now!

2. Ask and Answer

If you hold the balance of power—you're the boss, you're more senior, you're paying the bill, or whatever— it can be tempting to ask the questions but avoid answering them. Peter Block, who first introduced me to the idea of having conversations about *how* to work together, calls this exchange "social contracting." A contract is a mutual exchange of value. Without both give and take, it's not a contract. Asking the other person about how they'd like to work is already a powerful act. But it's not a Keystone Conversation unless you answer the questions too.

SAY THIS
Your Word & Phrase Toolkit

These are just prompts. Choose what feels most natural and helpful to you, and tweak however you like.

- I'm curious to hear your answer to this.

- And what else?

- Here's how I'd answer that.

- Here's a hard question, but I think it's helpful for us to answer it.

- What needs to be said that hasn't yet been said?

- That's powerful/useful/illuminating to hear.

- Right, mm-hmm, nice, uh-huh, OK, good, sure, yep, lovely. (I'm repeating these, because these signs of acknowledgment and encouragement are the lubrication of the Keystone Conversation.)

See me role-model a Keystone Conversation at BestPossibleRelationship.com, or follow the QR code.

At the End: Appreciate the Good

One of our brain's quirks is that it loves beginnings and endings. The primacy effect (we better remember the first things) and the recency effect (we better remember the last things) are cognitive biases, heuristics that Daniel Kahneman made popular in *Thinking, Fast and Slow*. The primacy effect is why in musical theatre the opening and closing numbers are so critical. Even if things are "soft" in the middle, with a rousing number at the end you literally and metaphorically finish on a high note, and everyone walks away feeling good.

Years ago, in Boston, I went with some friends to the House of Blues. It was a little perfunctory—you wouldn't make the mistake of thinking you were at a real blues club in Chicago—but I admired the cunning design. For the last song, they got us up on our feet to "feel the vibe" and lift the energy. When the song was done, our hearts were pumping... and they smoothly ushered us out so they could turn over the room for the next sitting. Now when I facilitate a training session or give a keynote, I often design it so that the crowd is on its feet at the end, less to reset the tables and more to end with the audience giving themselves a standing ovation and finishing the event on a high.

Too many important conversations end with a whimper. Even if the energy has been great, you've been brave and forthright, and you've covered important ground, ending the Keystone Conversation on an up beat will increase its impact.

DO THIS
1. Share the Learning

Set a precedent of making every conversation with you a learning one. Ask, "What was most useful here for you?" When you also answer that question, you do three things. First, you make tangible what was most helpful for you. By naming it and saying it out loud, you strengthen the wiring in your brain, making the most useful parts more memorable and precious. Second, you give the other person feedback about what worked best. They'll know what to do more of (and less of) in the next conversation. And finally, you confirm that this was in fact a useful conversation, one of many other useful or valuable conversations you'll have going forward.

2. Appreciate the Conversation

You've both taken a risk by having this conversation, and you've both indicated some commitment to a Best Possible Relationship. That's no small thing. You've started building a working relationship that's safe, vital, and repairable. Celebrate that. Appreciate that.

SAY THIS
Your Word & Phrase Toolkit

These are just prompts. Choose what feels most natural and helpful to you, and tweak however you like.

- Thank you, that was really helpful. I'm excited for what's ahead.

- What was most useful or most helpful for you?

- Here's what was most valuable for me.
- What do you know now that you didn't know before?
- I'm celebrating [insert what's true for you].
- I appreciate [insert what's true for you].

 See me role-model a Keystone Conversation at BestPossibleRelationship.com, or follow the QR code.

You've Made a Brilliant Start

You can't underestimate what a fantastic start you've made by having this Keystone Conversation. Seriously, it's a rare and brilliant thing not only to have created space and time but also to have modelled the curiosity and vulnerability required.

That's true, even if you feel like it didn't go well. I know, a paradox. But no matter if the conversation was a little weird, or you didn't hear or speak the answers you thought you would, or the vibe was different from what you expected, you've won. You opened the portal to a Best Possible Relationship. Now there's a shared commitment to something that matters, and a shared permission to talk again about how to keep succeeding. You've made this relationship's safety, vitality, and repairability matter.

But don't stop now. This isn't a "one and done" deal. Stay committed to this BPR's success with regular maintenance.

If you're speaking of love,

you really must include the element

of uncertainty—and perhaps

it's best approached as the art of

constant maintenance.

TWYLA THARP

Keep Your Best Possible Relationship Alive

The art and science of maintenance

Disintegration Is Inevitable

Billy Bragg, the Bard of Barking, sings, "I saw two shooting stars last night / I wished on them, but they were only satellites." It's now more than forty years since he wrote "A New England" and it's only got busier up in LEO—"low Earth orbit." About 1,400 satellites were launched in 2021 alone.

It's crowded up there, and where there's a crowd, there's trash. You might remember the scene from the movie *WALL-E* where a rocket leaving Earth bursts through a shell of space debris. This is the Kessler effect in glorious Pixar animation: space debris leads to more space debris, which creates a cascade of even more space debris. It only takes a very small piece of ex-satellite whizzing around at 15,000 miles/24,000 kilometres per hour to hit something and break it.

You Are in Orbit Too

You might not be moving at supersonic speed, but consider yourself in orbit with this other person with whom you're building a Best Possible Relationship. You're zipping around each other, independent but connected. What's more, you're constantly receiving minor damage from the simple give-and-take of everyday actions. A small ding here, a hiccup there, a minor flare-up. There might be bigger strikes too. Getting through everyday life without the occasional bruise? It's impossible.

That's why commitment to maintenance is essential. The Keystone Conversation is a brilliant start, but things deteriorate without regular upkeep. Run with whatever metaphor strikes your fancy: gardens need pruning and weeding; engines need fine-tuning and new oil; houses need cleaning and the occasional lick of paint; software needs to be debugged.

The coming pages help you establish a **maintenance schedule**. You'll see the small actions you might choose to do often, the necessary things you should do when a situation calls for it, and how to do the bigger, more difficult things when it comes to that.

We are not going to start with a list of tactics. We're going to begin with principles to shape what you do and how you show up, and that will underpin all your acts of maintenance.

Six Principles of Maintenance

Rushing to tactics is tempting. Who doesn't pause, even for a microsecond, at a headline like "The Seven Guaranteed Ways to Make Your Team Love You (Number Five Will Blow Your Mind!)"? But useful tactics only emerge when principles and context combine. Here's what *you* might do with *this* person in *this* situation. You'll bring the context, so let me suggest six principles that speak to the being and the doing of successful maintenance.

The first three principles are about the state of mind you bring to the everyday interactions of your Best Possible Relationship. They are underpinned by a call for openness, and I appreciate that's not a small ask. Under stress, we're wired to shut down, keep it small, and stay safe. These three principles will help you manage and override some deep wiring.

Stay curious.
Stay vulnerable.
Stay kind.
Adjust always.
Repair often.
Reset as needed.

Stay Curious

Whatever you think is going on, you're wrong. Not totally, but partially. Sure, you see some of the picture, but you don't see all of it by any means. Full-hearted, genuine curiosity dispels the fog that ambiguity or frustration will bring. Curiosity helps you understand the situation more deeply because it gets you out of your own head. It helps you maintain connection by more deeply seeing and understanding what's up for the other person, and it helps you better see how you are contributing to the challenge at hand. Be open-minded.

Stay Vulnerable

They also don't know what's going on, not fully. That's on them, and it's on you too. You're holding some things close to your chest: data, opinions, feelings, and what you want or need. Some of those things you explicitly know, and some of them are whispers, half-sensed and not yet fully articulated. Sharing can be illuminating for both of you. "I didn't know I thought/felt that until I said it out loud." Of course, oversharing can defeat the purpose—it's the flipside of hanging on to information for selfish reasons. Share what's useful for the Best Possible Relationship. Be open-handed.

Stay Kind

Towards the end of his life, the author Aldous Huxley wrote, "It's a bit embarrassing to have been concerned with the human problem all one's life and find at the end that one has no more to offer by way of advice than, 'Try to be a little kinder.'" This work is difficult, and doing it flawlessly is near impossible. You're doing your best, and they are probably trying hard too. Assume positive intent. Be generous. Remember that you're both committed to the Best Possible Relationship, and you can be kind to them and kind to yourself as you navigate that. Be open-hearted.

If you can be consistently open-minded, open-handed, and open-hearted, you bring a great gift to any working relationship. Those three principles are the very foundation of a Best Possible Relationship. The final three principles concern the rhythm of successful maintenance. There are daily, regular, and occasional interventions that incorporate actions both big and small.

Adjust Always

I'm no sailor, but it seems that managing a small boat in open water is yet another metaphor that describes the nuances of managing a relationship. You need to avoid the big disasters—hitting rocks, pirates, getting swamped, and so on. You also need to make the most of the conditions. You tap the tiller and trim the sails to adjust to the waves and the wind. It's all fine-tuning, just as it is with relationships. Conditions shift in relationships, and you need to adjust to what the moment requires.

Repair Often

My dad was an engineer, and he knew how to hammer, glue, and fix the little things that end up breaking around a house. I inherited *none* of that practicality. Instead, I got clumsiness, so I've a certain expertise around patching *myself* up. As I've bumped my way through life, I've collected scars. I've learned that when you get dinged, deal with it quickly. Bring the wound into the light because sunlight disinfects. Understand what's hurting and apply a salve.

Reset as Needed

I was in a mastermind group with four other people for nearly fifteen years. That's a long time. Our secret was that, on three different occasions, someone surfaced that the group had gone a bit flat, lost its zip, and we'd all started phoning it in. That gave us a chance to actively reset, change, and recharge the experience. The time we failed to do that, during a moment of stress, the group fatally broke apart. A BPR with any longevity will need some moments of reset to keep it safe and vital.

But before You Act, Orient

Before you can best act, it's helpful to know what's really going on. Your perspective is important, but it is by no means the whole picture. The next chapter shows you how to develop a more nuanced understanding of the drama that's currently unfolding.

Orient:
Know What's
Going On

In the era of Google, we've lost some of the magic and mystery of old-school maps. Now, getting somewhere just requires an app. I appreciate the efficiency, but I miss seeing the bigger picture and possible destinations. Can you imagine Bilbo Baggins typing "Lonely Mountain" into his cell phone and heading off?

When a working relationship becomes difficult, you might feel stuck and overwhelmed by what's going on. Afraid of what it means. Ashamed that it's happened. Angry at them for doing something disappointing and/or angry at yourself for the same reason. Taking a perverse joy at the sense of unfairness you're feeling.

You're "flooded," and your vision has literally and metaphorically narrowed: it seems like there's only one truth and one way to be (which, coincidentally, happens to be yours). But if you can step back and understand better what's going on, new options will emerge. That's why the United States Air Force colonel John Boyd's

OODA loop—Observe, Orient, Decide, Act—is one of the most long-lasting frameworks for managing yourself in conflict. In the heat of the battle, observe before you act.

Here are two "maintenance questions" to map the situation, better understand the landscape, and navigate towards any necessary maintenance and repair.

1. What Are the Facts?

A powerful model for understanding how *your* truth is not necessarily *the* truth stems from the work of Marshall Rosenberg and Nonviolent Communication. When you notice the swirl going on in your mind and heart, you can gain a calmer and more nuanced understanding of what's true by teasing apart the dynamics and sorting them into four buckets.

First, the **data**. These are the facts you can point at and say: this is true, this is a thing, this happened. It's what would get admitted to a court of law as evidence. When you seek the data, what's predictably surprising is that you discover far fewer facts than you expected.

Instead, you find a *lot* of opinions. This is the second bucket, **judgments**, also known as suggestions, points of view, interpretations, readings of the situation, advice, and "good ideas." This is the gift that keeps on giving, as you bend the data to your worldview. In a single situation you'll have opinions about three different factors: the other person ("They are..."), you and your role in this ("I am..."), and the situation as a whole ("This is...").

You can often link judgments and data with the word "because." "I am in big trouble [judgment] because the taxi isn't here [data]." "They're unreliable [judgment] because the report is two days past due [data]."

Your **feelings** are the third element in the mix. There are other helpful models, but I keep this simple and work with five core emotions: mad, sad, glad, ashamed, and afraid. Ironically, any sentence you utter that begins "I feel that..." is most likely a judgment.

Your feelings are entwined with your judgments. "I am sad because I am in big trouble because the taxi isn't here." "I am angry because they're unreliable because the report is two days past due."

The truth seems obvious enough when it's broken down like this. But the lived experience is more like: "My judgments are This; I'm unable to notice and/or articulate my feelings; and I'm not that interested in the data unless it proves my judgments." In other words, judgments, data, and feelings combine into an unholy cocktail of distorted understanding.

The fourth bucket contains **what you want**. This work is about building "adult-to-adult" relationships with the people in your life. That sounds good, but what does it mean exactly? At an abstract level it can be finding a way to coexist with someone, balancing your respective strengths and blind spots, your desires and your boundaries. At a practical level, it can mean asking for what you want, knowing that the answer might be no.

Most of us could benefit from developing the skill of asking for what we want. How do you articulate that, and ideally in a way that increases the odds that the want will be heard? That can require unlearning old assumptions, the two most common being "It's not my place to ask" and "They should already know what I want." Clarifying what you want often has the effect of cutting through the situation like a sword and the Gordian knot. Brené Brown says, "Clear is kind." It's kind to ask for what you want.

When you feel overwhelmed by a situation, pause, and break it into these four buckets. This discipline helps you understand what's true and what's being made up about what's true. It helps you understand your feelings so you can use them in service of the conversation, rather than your feelings hijacking it.

2. What Position Are You In?

Edgar Schein's work has been influencing mine for
more than twenty years. In his book *Humble Inquiry*,
I first learned about the idea of being "one up" or "one
down" relative to a person I was interacting with. Schein
talks about how giving advice puts us "one up"—and,
therefore, the other person "one down"—which is why
we so often resist advice, even when we've requested it.
The therapist Terry Real uses the same language when
talking about the dynamics of dysfunctional relationships, where one person is in the "one up" position
and the other is "one down."

"One up" might show up as being in control, "high
status," indifferent, directive, incurious, cold, angry,
impervious, passive-aggressive, and blaming; or as
having the explicit power, making the decisions, and
not trusting the other person. "One down" might show
up as being blamed, "low status," "victim-y," resigned,
complaining, desperate, manipulative, passive; as
having no explicit power and not trusting yourself.

In this particular relationship and at this particular moment, what position are you in? What's
powerful here is to step back and see the dynamic.

If a relationship is out of balance, someone will be "one up" and someone will be "one down." It's another pattern; it's another dance.

A New Perspective

The above two practices invite you out of yourself so you can (somewhat) objectively observe yourself and the situation. Noticing the dance you're dancing is instructive. It makes the dynamics seem less personal, and it also reveals that you have a role in what's going on. The two of you, in this moment, are creating the dynamics together.

With this wider, more systemic, and often more compassionate perspective, you can decide what's your best next step: to adjust, to repair, or to reset.

 Download a template to help you tease apart data, judgments, feelings, and wants (and get other resources) at BestPossibleRelationship.com, or follow the QR code.

Adjust Always: Give and ~~Take~~ Receive

Adam Grant's book *Give and Take* is one of my "top-shelf" books. I keep it where I can see it to remember its counterintuitive message: faced with the choice of being a giver, a taker, or a "matcher," the givers have *both* the least and the most successful outcomes. If you give without boundaries, you become a victim. If you give generously but sustainably, you flourish.

My twist on Grant's work is to suggest that while you don't want to become known as a "taker," you do want to be someone who can receive what's offered. To hark back to Peter Block and his idea of a social contract, there needs to be a mutual exchange. It doesn't work if it flows one way.

The psychologist John Gottman's idea of bids makes the giving and the receiving an everyday currency of interaction. A bid, "the fundamental unit of emotional connection," is any gesture, question, or interaction intended to reach out to the other person.

In *The Relationship Cure*, Gottman says that "bid by bid" we build better relationships.

Here are two maintenance questions: one you can ask the other person and one you can ask yourself. The answers will help you create bids you might give and receive, all in service of your BPR.

1. What's Working Well?

In *The Coaching Habit*, I introduced the question, "What was most useful for you?" as the Learning Question, the final question of seven. I love it because it's a little sneaky. Beyond the power of identifying what was helpful about the exchange, it also subtly frames the conversation as undeniably useful. You're not asking, "Was this useful?" You're saying, "This was useful. What was most useful?"

For a similar reason, regularly asking the question, "What's working well?" is a helpful contribution to any BPR conversation. I often begin with it, a deliberate move to counteract our human bias to dive right into what isn't going well. It's not, "Is anything working well?" but rather, "Things are working well. What should we highlight?"

When you ask that persistent and consistent question, it calms the nerves about a particular situation, and it strengthens the foundation of your BPR. Another of John Gottman's important research-based insights is that a relationship's likely resilience can be gauged by the ratio of positive interactions to negative ones. Five to one is the magic number. Noticing what's working well, asking what you're celebrating together, pointing to the good, and telling stories about your own small triumphs are all ways of adding to one side of that particular ledger.

2. What's the Quiet Gesture?

In *The Relationship Cure*, Gottman goes on to talk about "bid busters," the way we often turn down the other person's bid for connection. Sometimes we do this because we aren't paying attention. Because their bid is often subtle—a small wordless gesture, a seemingly inconsequential remark—we miss their attempt to build the bridge and connect. Sometimes, of course, we miss the bid because we're grumpy. We're not going to give them the satisfaction of turning the situation around.

When one of our bids gets turned down or ignored, we might feel downcast. It's a delicate moment, and we're often a bit fragile if it doesn't work. We don't think, "No matter, it's probably not personal; they were distracted or busy or whatever." We think, "That proves it. They hate me. I give up," or maybe, "Well, screw you if you don't care about this. I won't either. I give up" (or some less melodramatic but similar response).

The giving and receipt of a bid is a delicate process. If you're giving, keep giving. Try not to be downhearted if sometimes you're not heard. Stay alert to what the other person in your BPR is offering. They're giving to you all the time in small ways, in quiet gestures, offering small gifts and adjustments to keep your working relationship vital.

Adjusted

No matter how good the willingness to shine a light on what's working and the give-and-take of bids are, relationships still get dented. When they go a little off the rails—and things *always* go a little off the rails at some stage—you need to know how to repair what's been broken.

Repair Often: Manage the Damage

Climate change in Australia has brought about an increase in devastating fires. When the fires reach a certain size, they are untameable, and they travel with extraordinary and ruthless speed. Fires swept up to the outer suburbs of my hometown of Canberra in 2003, and the scars are still visible. In 2020 it happened again, and the skies turned orange with smoke and threat. Pre-emptive burning is one way to manage the danger. Using Indigenous wisdom stretching back tens of thousands of years, people burn off the undergrowth to remove the fire fuel. When the fires come, as they always do, there's less to burn.

Just as fires ignite in the Australian bush, so too will there be moments when your Best Possible Relationship is threatened. Sometimes pre-emptive work is required, sometimes you're dealing with a small flare-up, and sometimes the conflagration is bigger. An active commitment to repair maintains a BPR, and that requires you ensuring that a burn doesn't turn into longer-term damage.

Here are two maintenance questions to ask yourself to minimize the hurt.

1. What's As Yet Unsaid and Unsurfaced?

It's been a while since I've been afflicted with teenage acne, thank goodness. However, I remember clearly that while some pimples were loud, ugly, and obvious, the really painful ones were subterranean and elusive. It's a TMI metaphor for the moments when a threat to your BPR is dangerously hidden under the surface.

Sometimes you notice it in you. You're acting a little weird to yourself. You quite likely can't put your finger on it. But something's up. Sometimes you notice it in them. Something is off in their tone; they're not showing up quite how they do ordinarily.

You don't need to know *what's* wrong. You need to name that something might be wrong. "I'm noticing something feels off. What's up?" "What needs to be said that hasn't yet been said?" Sometimes there's a hurt to be healed, a minor transgression to be acknowledged and worked through. Sometimes, conflict is brewing.

2. How Will You Fight?

What's small has become big. What's quiet has become loud. You're now not just fixing damage, you're in explicit conflict. That's not terrible. Good conflict is healthy, or so we've all heard. But how do you fight with generosity and grace? It seems impossible. But in the Repair Question chapter, the Bridging exercise invited you to name the ways you already have some conflict skills. Books such as Amanda Ripley's *High Conflict*, Cinnie Noble's *Conflict Mastery*, and Douglas Stone, Bruce Patton, and Sheila Heen's *Difficult Conversations* suggest a range of tactics that can help. Don't try all of these at once. But look for the ones that will be most helpful to add to your repertoire.

Fundamentals
(which, make no mistake, are not easy)

- Breathe.
- Remember what success is. It's often not winning one particular fight. A so-called pyrrhic victory is when you win the immediate battle but the damage is so great you lose the war.

- Listen to understand what they want. They won't budge until they feel understood.

- Be as clear as you can about what you want. What is your request?

- Distinguish between data (what's fact) and judgments (yours and theirs).

- Concede when they have a point. Concede when they *possibly* have a point: "You might be right."

- Own your statements ("I am…"; "I feel…"; "I make up that…"). Avoid accusations ("You did…"; "You are…").

- Take a physical stance that's open rather than closed (whatever that means for you). I know it helps me to place my feet flat on the ground and to unclench my hands.

Advanced skills (which are harder still)

- Keep breathing.

- Abandon trying to prove that your version is The Truth. Liane Davey in *The Good Fight* says there are always two truths in an argument. Terry Real asks, in the battle to be right, "Who cares?"

- Be curious about what you and what they are defend-
ing. Something fundamental is at risk, beyond the
surface details. What's under threat is likely rooted
in Howard Markman's three core foci of conflict:
power and control, trust and closeness, and respect
and recognition.

- Say "I don't know" when you don't know. Sometimes,
say "I don't know" even when you kind of know.
This alone can stop an escalating conversation in
its tracks.

- See if they understood your point. "What do you
think I was saying then?" What will seem unambig-
uous and uncontroversial to you, they may interpret
wildly differently.

- Ask for a break if that would help the situation.
Sometimes a "time out" will benefit everyone.

Germination

Fire in Australia causes devastation. But not only devastation. Many eucalyptus species in Australia rely on a regular season of fire. Only the heat of a bushfire is sufficient to start the cycle of regeneration: seed pods are cracked open, seeds are released, they land on fresh ash-covered soil and root, and a healthy cycle of renewal begins again. At times we benefit from a moment of reset in our working relationships. It might not be the end; it might be a new beginning.

Reset as Needed: Ending (and Beginning)

When my dad was dying, I lived for a time in my childhood home with him and my mum. My parents were a loving couple, but now the relationship was being tested in a new way. Their preemptive grief meant they were both sad and afraid, no longer able to live their lives and run the house the way they had. The stress of the situation understandably brought some tension. Nothing terrible, but as their son I didn't want Mum's last memories of her relationship with Dad to have that edge.

I proposed that we work through a version of the Keystone Conversation. Suggesting this was in no way natural or easy. We've never particularly been a family for deep, introspective conversations. And who wants to facilitate their parents in a conversation like this? Not me, that's for sure.

My own resistance to this idea was minimal compared to my parents'. They were deeply unenthusiastic. But I'm persistent. Dad was the first to come around to it, and eventually Mum did too. Her reluctant agreement was exactly how many of us would feel: "OK, I guess I'm willing to do it. But do I need to be there?" (They were both brilliant in the conversation.)

There are various reasons to reset a relationship. Most obvious might be when you've gone through a crisis and you want to take things back to the studs and rebuild. But conflict is not required. Sometimes, the situation has changed significantly enough—a shift in role or status, for instance—that the two of you need to imagine a new BPR.

Sometimes, the problem is that there *hasn't* been clarifying conflict. Rather, you've settled into what Terry Real, in *Fierce Intimacy*, calls "stable ambiguity": although it's mediocre and uncertain, it's a smidge easier to keep going than to break up. Finally, sometimes the working relationship is ending, and you want to finish it as best you can with grace, appreciation, and dignity.

Here are two maintenance questions to help you navigate the end and explore new beginnings.

1. Should We Begin Again?

You'll remember that one power of a Keystone Conversation is that it sets a precedent for talking about how you work together. The state of health of your working relationship, a topic that often feels off limits, can be on the agenda.

After some sort of conflict, whether it's a small disturbance in the harmony or a more significant confrontation, the moment is ripe to reset the relationship with what is in effect another Keystone Conversation. Your initial plans have had a run-in with reality. You've still got the same shared commitment, but now you've got a bunch of new behaviours, patterns, and interactions to work through. Once again, you're seeking to answer this singular question: What do we need to know about each other so that we can reforge a BPR together?

You're at a crossroads. Avoid the reset, and the relationship will likely continue to deteriorate. Take the opportunity to plant the seeds of repair and recovery, and you'll strengthen it. You've already got tools you can use from the Keystone Conversation section. You might layer in these questions and ways of thinking.

Stay compassionate (towards them and you)

- How are you doing? Here's how I'm doing.

- I found that hard/difficult/upsetting/confusing. How did you find it?

Stay curious
(about how you ended up in this place)

- What's the data, and what did we both make up about what that meant?

- What spark set this off?

- What do you wish you'd done differently? Here's what I wish I'd done differently.

- How would we do a better job with something like this in the future?

Stay committed (to the BPR and to repair)

- What would you like to hear from me? Here's what I'd like to hear from you.

- What needs to be said that hasn't yet been said?

- What else is needed, so we can begin this again?

2. How Do We Finish This?

Sometimes the decision is not to begin again, but to finish the relationship. Its time is up: something may have been irremediably broken, or the arc may be complete. All things, BPRs as well, have their season.

We don't always get to choose how we depart. I've already mentioned Antigonus in *The Winter's Tale* ... exit, pursued by a bear, never to reappear, so that probably hasn't ended well. Luckily, you've got more options than Antigonus, so decide how you'd like it to end. Different circumstances will demand different responses, but if you can take the third option below as often as possible, you've had the good luck of and done the hard work for a BPR that's been something to celebrate.

The Ghost. You decide it's not worth the effort and you disappear without a trace. It's clean and neat on your end, and it's typically frustrating and confusing for the other person.

The Cortés. Spanish conquistador Hernán Cortés allegedly ordered his boats to be burnt upon arriving at the shores of the Aztec empire. There would be no going back. You may not have boats, but you've got bridges, although not for much longer. You decide that not only is there nothing worth saving here but you're also going to show some people *exactly* how you feel about the experience.

The Wake. The wake is a great Irish tradition to celebrate a death. There's sorrow and there's celebration. It's a deliberate gathering to talk about what's passed. It's generous, it's safe, it's celebratory. You can shape yours by using some of these questions.

- What's the best story you can tell about this BPR?

- What needs to be celebrated? What do you need to say thank you for?

- What have you learned? How have you changed and grown?

- What doesn't need to be said? What can you keep quiet?

- What does dignity look and sound like? How can both of you "save face"?

Ending

One of the most wonderful books I've read recently is *With the End in Mind* by Kathryn Mannix. She's a British doctor and cognitive behavioural therapist committed to helping people be less afraid of dying. She covers a lot of ground: most of us are unfamiliar with death and anxious about it, no matter whether we're at the end of our life or if someone who matters to us is dying.

Mannix tells sad and mostly joyful stories of how people come to a good death. Thinking about how we face the end of a relationship is not *quite* the same, but I suspect we can apply at least two things from her work. First, the unknown can be the scariest thing. We tend to catastrophize and think the worst; in fact, most endings are quieter and gentler than we realize. Second, it's helpful to actively manage the experience for all the players in the drama. Yes, hoping it will end well *sometimes* works . . . but the process will likely have more generosity, presence, and grace if you think about and shape what happens.

I feel very connected to you…

in love and catastrophe,

as if we are on

an adventure together.

NICK CAVE

We're Gloriously Entangled

This is a skill
for all your life

It's Relationships
All the Way Down

That the ways and means to work with people are lumped under the label of "soft skills" is a pet peeve of mine. We've got "hard skills" for logic, coding, strategy, and whatever; the rest of that mushy stuff we dismiss as "soft skills."

It's a tad insulting, and it's increasingly at odds with how actual scientists see the world. For a while now science has been pointing us away from units as the primary organizing factor of life. The interesting work isn't about things, about atoms. It's about the relationship between things.

Quantum mechanics—which the physics professor Carlo Rovelli has called "perhaps the most successful

Not every relationship is going to be fantastic. But every one could be better.

scientific idea ever. So far, it has never been proved wrong"—has started to frame properties of things in terms of how they are relative to other things. Rovelli puts it plainly when he writes that a good scientific theory "should not be about how things 'are,' or what they 'do': it should be about how they affect one another."

Quantum mechanics feels obscure to most of us, but it's not just in that realm that the focus on relationships is increasing. At a more human scale, authors like Peter Wohlleben (*The Hidden Life of Trees*) and Suzanne Simard (*Finding the Mother Tree*) describe how no tree is separate from the forest that surrounds it. Through the "wood wide web" of mycorrhizal fungi, trees talk to each other across distances, give and take resources from one another, and build agency about the future.

What's true for atoms and for trees is true for us. We are our relationships.

Not every working relationship is going to be fantastic. But nearly every one of your working relationships could be better. A commitment to build the Best Possible Relationship with each one of your key people is a commitment to increased success and happiness.

"Missing" Man Joins

Search Party

Looking for Himself

BBC WORLD NEWS

Bonus: Know Your Stuff

How to be wiser
about who you are

Sort Your Cards

My wife is a Canadian. And not just a Canadian but a daughter of Newfoundlanders. Having Newfoundland DNA means a number of things. You can tell a great story. You're deeply loyal to your friends. And you play a ferocious game of cards.

The first time I played cribbage on the East Coast, I was pitied, mocked, and thrashed in equal measures. I had no idea what I was doing, but it was clear: learn fast or die. Crib involves both pegging and rapid math (neither of which you need to worry about here). It also involves being able to quickly sort your hand. You're dealt six cards, and you must decide which four to keep and which two to discard.

This bonus section of the book is precisely that: a chance to better understand your hand and which cards are your best. It offers ways to deepen your understanding about who you are, how you show up, how you give, and how you receive.

For each of the five Keystone Conversation questions, I've provided two additional exercises to stretch your thinking and self-awareness. Some come at the question directly, some more obliquely.

Intrigued? I hope so.

Be curiously skeptical. When I do this work, I try not to be seduced into thinking that all my answers are The Truth. Sometimes, they're the first step towards a deeper insight. It's helpful to be a little skeptical about the process and equally so about your answers. Don't swallow them whole.

 I've got four ways to "triangulate" your answers and reality-check them. You'll also find them at BestPossible Relationship.com, or follow the QR code.

A Deeper Dive on the Amplify Question

The quest for the "most" of any colour has literally and metaphorically intensified in recent years. It started with Vantablack, a black so black that it absorbs 99.96 percent of light. You've never used it, and nor will you, because sculptor Anish Kapoor has managed to claim exclusive rights to using it in art. If that seems selfish, Stuart Semple agrees. He's developed Black 3.0 in response to Vantablack, and anyone in the world *except* Kapoor can use it.

In recent years Semple developed the pinkest pink and, in late 2021, the whitest white. Inspired by such diverse sources as the ghost beetle and plant luminescence, White 2.0 is made from a mixture of high-quality pigments, resins, optical brighteners, and mattifiers, which combined reflect 99.98 percent of light. Semple says that White 2.0 is 50 percent brighter than the bestselling white paint.

When you show up at and as your best, you get to shine more brightly than before. The first of these exercises draws on different archetypes to help you articulate your best, while the second one calls in the help of a friend.

EXERCISE
Archetypes

The Hero's Journey has such resonance not just because of the nature of the journey: crossing the threshold, journeying through danger and challenge, facing and mastering the hard thing, and journeying back. It's also because a range of familiar characters are always part of the adventure.

The hero carries the weight of the quest on her shoulders. It's down to her to keep moving along the path and make the decisive move. The mentor is a teacher and a guide, someone with hard-earned wisdom.

They're willing to share their scars and stories. The ally has the hero's back, often chopping wood and carrying water so the hero can do what she needs to do. The ally is a cheerleader and a resource. The shapeshifter adapts to what's required, and can fit in or stand out as needed. They're adaptable and elusive.

For the first part of this exercise, ask yourself which role you are most comfortable playing, the role you most often default to. Is there one you aspire to? What role might the other person most usefully play?

Interacting with those four roles are four energies. As I wrote in *How to Begin*, this wisdom comes from First Nations communities in North America, along with the ritual of "calling in the energies" at the start of a gathering. The four energies are those of the warrior (boundaries, a line in the sand, engaging with conflict, fierce protection); the healer or lover (comfort, care, recovery, healing, gentle protection); the teacher or magician (knowledge, learning, wisdom, details, exploration, experience); and the ruler or visionary (ambition, ruthlessness, big picture, strategy, clarity).

Which energy do you most naturally embody or most easily summon? Which ones feel more elusive and so you rely on others to bring them?

_____

_____

_____

_____

_____

_____

_____

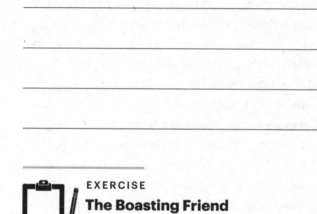

EXERCISE

The Boasting Friend

You're awesome... and you're doing great.

This is my email sign-off, and my mum hates it.
She _loathes_ it.

Not only is it too "Californian" for her by being over-the-top affirmation-y. But it is not grammatically correct.

"You're doing great," she'll say. "Do you mean, 'You're doing well'? You're a Rhodes Scholar, for goodness' sake!"

She's technically correct about the grammar. But what I know and she doesn't is that every week I get an email or three saying words to the effect of, "Thanks for the encouraging note. I needed to see that."

Most of us get squirmy articulating the best of who we are, and for two main reasons. First, most of us are a little fuzzy about what choice words will express the very best of who we are. A second and more significant barrier is that even if we have some inkling of what makes us great, we are unwilling to name it out loud. We don't want to be that self-promoting, attention-stealing, credit-claiming blowhard who assumes that the top of the mountain is naturally theirs.

Here's a cunning way to get past your own modesty and to find the words to express your technical, emotional, and relational strengths.

Imagine I'm speaking with one of your best friends. I ask them, "What is it that you, [the name of your best friend], really appreciate about [your name, dear reader]?" I go on, "Can you put aside the jokey or snarky or sarcastic comments for a moment," which, after all, in many cultures is an expression of love, "and give it to me straight? What do they do? What about who they are do you most deeply appreciate? Tell me five things, or more."

What would your best friend say?

This exercise helps you sidestep the awkwardness of yakking on about your own great qualities. That's uncomfortable for most of us. Putting yourself in the third person and imagining someone else talking about you feels more objective and impersonal. When you see yourself through another's eyes, you often see things that you might not have noticed before.

_____

_____

_____

_____

_____

_____

A Deeper Dive on the Steady Question

René Magritte painted a picture of a pipe and wrote underneath it, "*Ceci n'est pas une pipe.*" When he says "This is not a pipe," he's making explicit the way we categorize and so simplify and reduce what we sec. The painting is called *The Treachery of Images*, and it's a reminder that the labels we give things around us are only ever rough guides and not the truth.

But we love a good label. They're helpful, of course. Humans are creatures of patterns and habits, and when we name something, it tells us how to navigate it. When you did the Deep Read Me exercise in the Steady Question chapter, you were figuring out labels you'd

like to share ("I'm not *really* a procrastinator... but
I work best under pressure"). And when you talk about
that in the Keystone Conversation, your pre-existing
labels for the other person are confirmed or refined.

But using labels is a flirtation with danger. Their
descriptions are limited, and labels are sticky. These
exercises can bring more nuance and complexity
to labels you've already named for yourself. The first
exercise invites you to add context and story. The
second one breaks through binaries to offer some
choices on a spectrum.

EXERCISE

Where Did You Learn Your Work Habits?

In your first year or two working as a young adult,
you're starting to understand what you've let yourself
in for. Just what is this whole "adulting" thing? High
school (and university if you went there) felt hard
enough. But a full-time job... "Wait, I have to get up
and do it all again? And for another forty years?" It's a
bit of a shock to the system.

Steve Morrow champions coaching and leadership at Salesforce, a company that generates more than $25 billion in revenue a year. I spoke with him about how they think about building better relationships, and one of the questions they ask is, "Where did you learn your work habits?"

I've shamelessly stolen it. The brilliance of that question is that habits are, by definition, unconscious: we've stopped noticing them. In this exercise, notice a few of your key work habits, and use them as a springboard to backfill the story of what you've learned, where you learned it, and why you decided that it was important. It might be about work preferences, about how you show up in working relationships, about how you manage stress or conflict, or indeed any of your "This is just how I do it" ways of working.

If it's helpful, use this formula: I [work like this] because I've learned [story of when you learned this preference].

_____

_____

_____

_____

EXERCISE
Calm or Volatile?

A digital world gives us such a neat choice. It's either 1 or 0, black or white, on or off. That works for algorithms, but it's rarely enough to describe our human complexity. Yes, some of our choices are binary, and you answered some of those questions in the core Steady Question exercise ("Do you prefer your Zoom camera on or off?").

A messier and to my mind more interesting exercise can be to understand a deeper type of preference, one that points to more fundamental currents of behaviour. Because these choices exist less literally and more metaphorically ("Are you more in the spotlight or in the wings?"), the answers are not one or the other. Rather, they are more about understanding the "prizes and punishments" of certain polarities, and where your preference might be located on the spectrum in between.

For me, there's no value judgment in the endpoints of spectrums. For instance, I see value in both "calm" and "volatile." But you may find some words work better than others or don't work. Feel free to build your own spectrums, the ones that are most helpful to describe you in all your glory.

Where would you put yourself along these spectrums? Are you more...

One of the crowd	I I I I I I I I I I I	Soloist
Settled	I I I I I I I I I I I	Agitated
Meandering	I I I I I I I I I I I	Direct
Rhythm section	I I I I I I I I I I I	Lead guitar
Sustainer	I I I I I I I I I I I	Disruptor
Listener	I I I I I I I I I I I	Talker
Certainty-lover	I I I I I I I I I I I	Adventurer
[_____]	I I I I I I I I I I I	[_____]

A Deeper Dive on the Good Date Question

One of my favourite paintings in the National Gallery in London is *The Arnolfini Portrait* by Jan van Eyck. A couple stand full length, forefront in a Flemish room. The husband is wearing a huge hat, Jamiroquai-style (for those of you who rocked in the 1990s), and a long dark coat trimmed with fur. He holds the hand of his new wife, who wears a flowing green velvet dress. Behind the woman is a four-poster bed in luxurious red, an impressively spiky chandelier hangs from the ceiling, a cute little dog looks up from the bottom of the picture, and on the back wall is a round mirror.

It's the mirror I love. In it is a tiny portrait of van Eyck himself. It's a timeless reminder that even as you've held up the mirror to yourself, there's another gaze to account for: the other person.

Van Eyck's masterpiece points to a deeper truth: interdependence is essential to life. Self-knowledge is nothing until you test it in the arena of your relationships. The spiritual leader Ram Dass summed it up perfectly: "If you think you're enlightened go spend a week with your family."

These two exercises deepen your understanding of why a previous relationship was strong and nourishing. You've already explored what you and they did and said that made it so. This is a chance to dig deeper.

EXERCISE
How Did They Love You?

I resisted reading Gary Chapman's *The 5 Love Languages* for *years*. I felt like it would be the worst of all self-help books, a bias only reinforced by the 1980s-style Harlequin Romance cover. So, I was wrong. It's a simple, helpful model. Our love language is how we like to be appreciated. The five options are: words of affirmation (saying supportive things); acts of service (doing helpful things); receiving gifts (giving thoughtful gifts); quality time (spending meaningful time); and physical touch (being close).

People often tend to "give" in the language that they best like to receive. That's extremely helpful: How do they express appreciation? Right, that's how they probably like to be appreciated. But be aware that it can be a blind spot too: Here's how I like to be appreciated, so surely that's how they like to be appreciated.

In this exercise, identify the love language that most lights you up. Now reflect on past successful relationships, and notice what forms of appreciation particularly struck a chord with you. What can you glean about how you give and how you receive appreciation?

_____

_____

_____

_____

EXERCISE
Hide & Seek

If you're a British "twitcher"—a mad keen bird watcher—you'll be familiar with hides: disguised huts or "blinds" where you can stay hidden while observing the bird action (if "action" is not too strong a word). It seems that many of us retreat to hides in our working lives too. You'll remember the Deloitte study I referenced earlier that discussed how almost two-thirds of employees downplay parts of their identity.

This exercise is called Hide & Seek because it's about naming your gifts and then sharing about when you might hide them and when you might bring them forth.

Start with your gifts. You'll have made good progress on this already if you did the Boasting Friend exercise. Answer questions such as, What are your best contributions? What are you known for? What *should* you be known for? Your gifts likely draw on some combination of your technical expertise, your experience and lessons learned, your preferences and those things you're naturally wired to do, and the way you work with others.

Once you see your gifts, explore how you hide them in some relationships and how, in the best relationships, you've found a way to bring them into the light. In what moments do you doubt yourself and retreat from the light? What's going on in those moments you decide to stay silent and not contribute? What allowed you to share your gifts, to get some early wins, to bring the best of yourself to the work at hand?

The import of this exchange reminds me of the lines from W.B. Yeats's poem "Aedh Wishes for the Cloths of Heaven":

I have spread my dreams under your feet;
Tread softly because you tread on my dreams.

It's a delicate and precious gift to you both.

_____

_____

_____

_____

_____

_____

_____

_____

A Deeper Dive on the Bad Date Question

t's been a while since I've heard hackers labelled as a white, grey, or black hat, with each shade of chapeau implying a different level of ethics and morality. The term is from a more innocent age—you know, five or six years ago—before we fully realized that we were victims of our own social media algorithms, that countries were mucking around with other countries' elections, and that blackmailers' preferred method of payment is cryptocurrency.

We imagine that in old-school Westerns, the outlaws always wore the black hats and the good guys the white ones. Although the costumes were never really that clear cut, an iconic movie moment happens at the end of 1903's *The Great Train Robbery*. One of the robbers faces the camera and fires his six-shooter at the audience. He wears a black hat.

In the UK, the villain also wears a black hat: not a Stetson, but more likely a top hat. In the tradition of pantomime, our baddie enters stage right—the rest of the cast enters stage left—and his arrival is a cue for the audience to boo, hiss, and shout, "He's behind you!"

And the most famous black hat of recent times is a helmet. (Think asthmatic breathing, father issues, and light sabres.)

Talking about frustrating, broken, and failed relationships is a powerful act of vulnerability. It strengthens trust immediately and makes it more likely that both of you will be able to navigate the tougher moments when they inevitably come to this working relationship. The first of these exercises puts the black hat on the other person; the second one gives you a chance to firmly claim the black hat for yourself.

EXERCISE
What Do People Get Wrong about You?

In his podcast *The Knowledge Project,* Shane Parrish interviewed leadership coach Randall Stutman. Stutman reflected on one of the most revealing questions to ask:

When you meet people for the first time, what do they get wrong about you? What do they misperceive about you? What do they overestimate about you, underestimate about you? What do they just get wrong?

For Stutman, the answer will reveal a level of self-awareness (or not) that's helpful to understand. How wise is this person to the nuances of their presence in the world?

For me, this question has a "three insights for the price of one" impact. First, to Stutman's point, it's a way to view yourself from the outside and to notice how you present to the world. It disrupts your own self-certainty about your lived experience. Second, you can then tell the other person in your Keystone Conversation about ways in which you are under- or overestimated. In the next section, there's a similar but different exercise about this (Is That a Cigar?).

But the deepest insight is that your answers reveal the gap between how you judge yourself (by your intentions) and how you judge others (by their actions). This bias is why we often have a more elevated sense of ourselves than others have of us. If things don't work out exactly as planned (and let's face it, when do things ever work out exactly as planned?), at least you know your intention was good. But when others screw up, you don't have access to their intentions, so the proof of the pudding is in what you know they've done or not done. So, your answers can make you more curious about the gap between intentions and the perception of actions, both yours and others.

So, what do people get wrong about you? And, if you'd like to go deeper, what's the kernel of truth about who you are that is at the heart of their misperceptions?

_____

_____

_____

_____

_____

_____

_____

EXERCISE
Claim Your Villain

    This is your chance to grab your black hat of choice and claim it loudly and proudly. Here are seven essential villainous moves, with a fictional role model for each. In this exercise, name the top two or three moves that you've pulled off over the years. (Answering "none of the below" is not an option.)

- Betrayal (I'll break my promises ... e.g., Macbeth)

- Neglect (I'll ignore you; you're not worthy of my time ... e.g., Miss Havisham)

- Smothering (I'll keep you in the cage ... e.g., the witch in "Hansel and Gretel")

- Temptation (I'll take you off your path... e.g., Darth Vader)

- Obsession (I'll let nothing get in the way of my goal... e.g., Captain Ahab)

- Bullying (I'll put you in your place... e.g., Dolores Umbridge)

- Destruction (I'll destroy what you build and who you are... e.g., President Snow)

Now, if you were an actor in the same vein as Daniel Day-Lewis, you'd want to understand the motivation for the behaviour. Is it about insecurity and whether you're up to the job? Is it about feeling your status or ambition is under threat? Maybe you've found yourself in victim mode, and you want others to suffer as you are. Perhaps a neediness is at the root of it.

Hopefully you don't recognize yourself in *all* these archetypal moves. But equally, don't claim that you never play one or more. The question to sit with is this: If you had to pick one of these villain roles as yours, which would it be? Think of a time when you were under stress. In those moments, bad behaviour often shows up.

A Deeper Dive on the Repair Question

I n World War I, an American battalion was trapped behind enemy lines. Their perilous position became even more so when their own side started to shell them. They had to get a message across the lines. But how? Without radio, the signal corps relied on trained pigeons to carry the message. The first bird was released and immediately shot and killed by a German sniper. A second one met the same fate. The final pigeon, Cher Ami, was the last hope.

It was thrown up into the air, and it took its bearings and started the perilous journey. The sniper shot and hit the bird. But this time the bird kept flying. Badly wounded, Cher Ami nevertheless made it to HQ, the message was passed along, the connection was re-established, and the battalion survived. Cher Ami was blinded and lost a leg but lived. In celebration of its heroic flight, the bird was awarded the Croix de Guerre and was eventually stuffed and displayed at the Smith-sonian in Washington, DC.

In the Bridging exercise in the Repair Question chapter, the focus is on the "pigeon." How do you cross the battleground and reforge a broken connection? These two exercises focus more on the dangers facing the pigeon. The first one helps you become more aware of what actions might inadvertently damage your rela-tionship, and the second one helps you understand your stress response; a response that can be misinterpreted and then exacerbate the initial dent in the relationship.

EXERCISE

Is That a Cigar?

Sigmund Freud was well known for picking apart dreams, looking for symbols. A smooth-walled house? That represents a man. A house with balconies good for, say, clinging? Probably a woman. Vermin?

Something to do with children, most likely. But even Freud had to admit that sometimes a cigar is just a cigar.

To dig into this exercise, review past misunderstandings, times when people have seemingly misinterpreted something you've done. Identify the misunderstandings that seem to reoccur, because it's a fair guess that they will again in the future too. When has the reaction seemed outsized to you? Make explicit what happens, what you think it means, and how your actions are taken the wrong way.

Your responses to other people's actions are often hot buttons of misinterpretation. You're silent, or you ask questions, or you don't ask questions, or you crease your brow, or you raise your eyebrows, or you ask for data, or you go off on a tangent. You don't even think about it: it's just what you do. But for the other person, these responses are loaded and triggering.

The misinterpretation probably is centred on Howard Markman's trilogy of power and control, trust and closeness, and respect and recognition. Do people think you're looking to hold on to control, to push them away, or to lessen them in some way?

Use this structure if it's helpful: When I do/say [x], it means [this] and rarely [this].

The misunder-
standings that
occurred in the
past will reoccur
in the future.

―――――――――――――――

That will work for you as you do this exercise, and you can use it again, if you wish, in the Keystone Conversation.

_____

_____

_____

_____

_____

EXERCISE
Stressed Out

When things go badly, your primitive brain and body decide how to react well before the rational mind is even aware of what's going on. Your heartbeat and blood pressure increase, your pupils dilate, your shoulders rise up as your body tenses, and you hold your breath.

You're getting ready for one of three main responses—and you'll have heard of at least two of these before: fight or flight. There's some debate on what to call the third one, but I like Terry Real's suggestion of fix.

Fight considers attack the best form of defence. It can be loud and messy; it can be cold and mean. Flight is about withdrawal. Sometimes that's physical; often it's present but walled off and checked out. The "freeze" response is folded into the flight response. And fix is "rescuer mode," taking all the responsibility for making things better, often with an unhealthy dose of self-immolation.

You'll have a preferred, practised response. In this exercise, map your typical response under stress. Go beyond the fight, flight, or fix labels. How do you act, specifically? Do you attack, and if so, what does that look like? Is it loud and large, or is it quiet and sneaky? Do you disappear, and what does that mean? Do you ghost, or do you start phoning it in and behaving passively aggressive? Or do you get paralyzed? Do you start lashing out and blaming others? Do you offer yourself up as a sacrifice, doing anything to make it "better"? Do you seem to get stupid, or quiet, or try to get out of the spotlight?

Mutually sharing this information in your Keystone Conversation offers the added bonus of being able to notice someone's stress-response behaviour ("Huh, they're in 'fix-it' mode"). You can point to what's going on ("I'm noticing...") and ask about it ("Is there anything stressing you out right now?").

_____

_____

_____

_____

_____

_____

_____

"Since when," he asked,

"Are the first line and last

line of any poem

Where the poem begins and ends?"

SEAMUS HEANEY

The Juicy Bits at the End

Common Questions about the BPR

How to Go Further and Deeper

Resources and Research

Thank You

Common Questions about the BPR

Yogi Berra, baseball philosopher, is credited with saying, "In theory, theory and practice are the same. In practice, they aren't." (In a perfect twist, in practice he didn't actually say that.) Having read through the theory, no doubt you have questions about how this might work with you and your people and in your context. I don't have all the answers, but here's my best shot.

Does this ever get easier and less awkward?
Yes, it does. As you learn the subtleties of what to ask and what to answer, and how to sit with the difficulty

of making relationships better, you become more relaxed and more skillful. But it's always work, and it always takes courage.

Does the dysfunction go away?

Hahahahaha. Oh wait, seriously? No, dysfunction, disappointment, and frustration are part and parcel of human relationships. Surely, you've looked at couples and thought, "What *is* going on there? Is that healthy or is it broken?" But the dysfunction is often diminished and more easily managed when you commit to the Best Possible Relationship.

Does this work for every relationship?

No, it doesn't. Hence the "almost" in the title of this book. It requires both parties to invest to some degree. Assuming you're serious about it, the other person also has to want to make it work, or at least must not actively disregard whether it works or not. But people will care more often than you might expect. Sure, some will be manipulative, entitled, self-obsessed, and utterly indifferent. But most people want the Best Possible Relationship.

It's also important to acknowledge the power differential in many relationships. Sometimes that's hierarchical—a boss and their direct report—and sometimes different societal factors come into play: gender, race, age difference, and so on.

I realize that sometimes these are insurmountable. I also believe that the BPR Keystone Conversation is one of the ways to lessen power differentials and make it easy to build "adult-to-adult" relationships.

I'm right at the start of my career. Can I do this?

You can definitely begin doing this right away. This is such a powerful idea that the sooner you start, the faster you move through incompetence to competence. I have to say, though, that it's going to be easier if you've had some experience of the good, the bad, and the ugly of working relationships. When you start working, you're (usefully, powerfully) optimistic and naïve. This work becomes more grounded if some of that has been rubbed away.

Will this work with my boss?

Often but not always. Some bosses will be delighted that you'd like to design a BPR together. Many will be slightly wary and confused because no one will have done this with them before. And some won't be in the least bit interested. Personally, when I've had that final type of boss, I've ended up trying to find a new role or job.

Can I have a BPR with someone I don't like?

Definitely. In fact, this is one of the best "use cases" for a BPR. You can muddle through mostly with people you like. But when you're working with someone with whom you don't "click," how do you give it the best chance of success and make it the least bad it can be? You work the BPR process with them.

Can I just ask the questions but not answer them?

I talk about this in the main part of the book, but it bears repeating: don't just ask the questions. If you do that, you significantly lessen the chance that this will be a BPR. At the heart of a BPR is a degree of shared openness and vulnerability, an exchange that feels equal enough on both sides. If the vulnerability is on one side only, the relationship will struggle to be as safe, vital, and repairable as it could be.

What if they're deluded about who they are?

Well, we're all slightly deluded. But let's assume they're *way* deluded. That makes things harder, for sure. But building the BPR closes that gap a little. There's an opportunity to say something like, "You said you'd do this, and now you're doing that. Why is that?" Hopefully, we all get wiser about who we are and how we work with others as part of this process.

How long does a Keystone Conversation take?

Aim for longer than ten minutes and shorter than thirty. "Your mileage may vary," as they say in the adverts, and it all depends on the other person and context.

How do I know if it's worked?

Way back on page 14, I talked about how success in a Keystone Conversation is more subtle than you'd expect. I believe what's most powerful about this process is that it gives permission to keep talking about the health of the relationship. Whatever the answers in the Keystone Conversation, you unlock the ability and share a commitment to do maintenance on the relationship.

How to Go Further and Deeper

MBS.works: unlock greatness

We offer the confidence, community, and programs to help you unlock your greatness and the greatness of others. We help you work better with other people, and bring out their best. We teach the practical tools from *The Coaching Habit*, *The Advice Trap*, and *How to Work with (Almost) Anyone*.

We help you find your next big thing. Based on *How to Begin*, we have a program to help you find and start your own Worthy Goal (something thrilling, important, and daunting) and a community called The Conspiracy to help you find the support and encouragement to work on it.

Box of Crayons: get curious about your *real* organizational challenges

Box of Crayons believes curiosity-led cultures are more resilient, innovative, and successful.

We are a learning and development company that helps organizations transform from advice-driven to curiosity-led.

Box of Crayons offers programming based on frameworks from the bestselling books *The Coaching Habit* and *The Advice Trap*. We partner with large-scale companies to help participants practise curiosity by asking more and better questions while resisting the urge to give advice, along with a step-by-step process for tackling real challenges from this foundation.

 Download the whitepaper "From Troublemaker to Changemaker: How to Harness Curiosity to Build Resilience and Innovation," which highlights the awesome organizational outcomes of curiosity. Learn more at BoxOfCrayons.com, or follow the QR code.

Resources and Research

Here are my favourite resources that I drew upon and learned from as I wrote this book.

On self-awareness and personal growth

Brené Brown, *Atlas of the Heart: Mapping Meaningful Connection and the Language of Human Experience.* Apparently there are a *lot* more feelings than the five I most typically articulate.

Susan David, *Emotional Agility: Get Unstuck, Embrace Change, and Thrive in Work and Life.* Susan's a great teacher, and I loved her conversation on Brené Brown's podcast.

Dick Richards, *Is Your Genius at Work? 4 Key Questions to Ask before Your Next Career Move*. Full of helpful exercises to figure out what you're great at.

Daniel Siegel, *Mindsight: The New Science of Personal Transformation*. The first book to make me consider therapy. How he talks about all the different integrations that are possible is provocative and helpful.

On relationship dynamics

Robert Bolton, *People Skills: How to Assert Yourself, Listen to Others, and Resolve Conflicts*. Now over forty years old, slightly stuffy to read, but full of essential truths.

Gary Chapman, *The 5 Love Languages: The Secret to Love That Lasts*. Helpful insights on appreciation that works.

Robin Dunbar, *Friends: Understanding the Power of Our Most Important Relationships*. "Dunbar's number" is 150—the number of relationships we can manage. This is Dunbar explaining why (and why 150 is not the only number that matters).

John Gottman, *The Seven Principles for Making Marriage Work: A Practical Guide from the Country's Foremost Relationship Expert* and *The Relationship Cure:*

A 5 Step Guide to Strengthening Your Marriage, Family, and Friendships. Research-backed insights on what it actually takes to create success.

Adam Grant, *Give and Take: Why Helping Others Drives Our Success.* Science-based understanding of how healthy reciprocity can work.

Esther Perel's podcasts *How's Work?* and *Where Should We Begin?* I love hearing relationships change and evolve during her sessions. And her "Where should we begin?" game is pretty great as well.

Philippa Perry's columns in *The Guardian* newspaper. She is firm and kind and has a gift for putting her finger on some of the more subtle dynamics.

Terrence Real, *Us: Getting Past You & Me to Build a More Loving Relationship.* The book is good, but his online training is even better, I think.

On conflict, fighting, and resolution

Liane Davey, *The Good Fight: Use Productive Conflict to Get Your Team and Organization Back on Track.* Particularly helpful for understanding that conflict can be a helpful part of team growth and organizational success.

Judith Hanson Lasater and Ike K. Lasater, *What We Say Matters: Practicing Nonviolent Communication*. The best book I've found on making Marshall Rosenberg's framework practical.

Cinnie Noble, *Conflict Mastery: Questions to Guide You*. The OG for conflict management coaching and mediation.

Amanda Ripley, *High Conflict: Why We Get Trapped and How to Get Out*. Offers practical tools for de-escalation.

Douglas Stone, Bruce Patton, and Sheila Heen, *Difficult Conversations: How to Discuss What Matters Most*. Best known for their seminal work on how to have feedback conversations.

 You can get a download of the list of "top-shelf" books I've recommended from this and all my previous books at BestPossibleRelationship.com, or follow the QR code.

Thank You

Thank you to Marcella. You are my best relationship and my best reader. Your guidance and encouragement have shaped this book, as with all my others.

Thank you to the MBS.works team. We're creating something special here, and I'm grateful for your help. Thank you, Ainsley, Amanda, Audra, Cindy, Claudine, Jessica, Sarah C., Sarah N., and Tugba.

Thank you to the Box of Crayons team. It's been extraordinary to watch you continue to flourish and grow since I've stepped away. A particular thank you to Dr. Shannon Minifie, Box of Crayons' wonderful CEO.

Thank you to my sparring partners, Dr. Jason Fox, Courtney Hohne, and Kate Lye. Your feedback in particular was fundamental to making this book better.

Thank you to the team at Page Two. This is now my fourth book with this wonderful organization, and I do think they are the role model for the very best of the publishing industry. If you have a book idea that's part of a bigger game, this might be the team for you. A particular thank you to my editor Kendra Ward; my designer Peter Cocking; my copy editor Jenny Govier; sales maestro Lorraine Toor; operations whizzes Gabi Narsted, Caela Moffet, Melissa Kawaguchi, and Rony Ganon; marketeers Maddie Taylor and Meghan O'Neill; and the founders, Trena White and Jesse Finkelstein.

I tried an experiment with this book: crowd-sourcing feedback on an early draft. It was all a bit overwhelming, but extraordinarily useful. Thank you to the MANY early readers of the second draft, who firmly nudged this to being a completely different book (and I'm crossing my fingers I've got everyone here who contributed).

Aileen Coombe, Ainsley Brittain, Alberto Cabas Vidani, Alejandro Reyes, Alex Czekalla, Alexandra Lise, Alison Parrin, Allison Allen, Allison Dell, Amanda Gavigan, Amber Caso, Andi Cuddington, Andrea Gomez-Ifergan, Andrea Hannah, Andrea Miller, Andrea Wanerstrand, Andrew Cromwell, Andrew Dolan, Andrew Kilshaw, Andrew Stotter-Brooks, Angela

Quinn, Anjana Bhaskaran, Ann Schulte, Barb Haines, Barbara Ann Shepard, Ben Widdowson, Benjamin Wipperman, Beri Meric, Beth Thompson, Betsy Dugas, Bill Brennan, Blair Steinbach, Bob Huff, Bonita Lane, Brad Field, Brenda Ammon, Britta Christiansen, Bruce Morgan, Calvin Strachan, Cara Williams, Carole Hackett, Carolina Figueredo, Caroline Gwynne, Caroline Schein, Carolyn Jones, Carolyn Reimer, Carolyn Richardson, Carolyn Taylor, Cathy Allen, Chantal Thorn, Cheryl Lower, Cheryl Naylor, Chris Hagen, Chris Lubrano, Chris Taylor, Christina Frowein, Christina Watt, Christopher Peter Makris (CPM), Cindy Snyder, Cinnie Noble, Claudine Plesa, Conni LeFon, Courtney Hohne, Dan Bigonesse, Dan Pontefract, Dane Jensen, Darci Hall, Darryl Wright, Dave McKeown, Dave Stachowiak, David Baldwin, Deborah Aurianivar, Deborah Hartmann, Deborah Sikkema, Debra Brooks, Debra Taylor, Derek Hill, Deseri Garcia, Dimitra Giatsi, Donald MacRae, Ed Sullivan, Eileen Cooke, Elena Holtham, Emily Lundi Mallett, Emily O'Toole, Emma Aylett, Erin Blanding, Evan Smith, Frank Monteleone, Frank Nguyen, Gabrielle Martinovich, Garry Ridge, George Kralidis, German Durand, Gina Rogers, Gladys Brignoni, Greg Deitz, Greg Thomas, Gus Stanier,

Gwenydd Jones, Heinrich Scharp, Helen Naoumov, Hélène Bellerose, Howard Parsons, Iain Milne, Jacob Morgan, Jake Redding, Jan de Zwarte, Jane Ruthford, Janet Weinstein, Jason Chickosis, Jason Ewert, Jason Fox, Jason Philibotte, Jeanette Thomas, Jeanine Delay, Jeff Gill, Jeff Raab, Jenica Veenstra, Jenn Krueger, Jenna Minifie, Jerry Klems, Jesper Thorson, Jesse Sostrin, Jill Murphy, Jo Stephenson, Joe Ilvento, Joe Whittinghill, John Mattone, Jon Nastor, Jonathan Hill, Jorge Giraldo, Joshua Gold, Jowi Taylor, Joyce Kristjansson, Julianna Morris, Julie Clow, Karen Eisenthal, Karen Hunt, Kasia Seremet, Kate Brown, Kate Lye, Kathy Johnson, Kay Aurand, Kelly Drewery, Kelly Kunzman, Kelly Pereira, Keturah Hallmosley, Kevin D. Wilde, Kevin Kernohan, Kimiko Mainprize, Klaus Krauter, Kris Jensen, Kristen Roberts, Kristin Caldwell, Kyla Devereaux, L.J. Viau, Laun Ruttenberg, Laura Gassner Otting, Laurie Sanci, Lenka Kotousova, Lesley Hayes, Leslie Watts, Linda Mallory, Lindsay McMurray, Lisa Fox, Lisa Hughes, Lisa Sretenovic, Lisa Wallace, Lisa Zarick, Liz Broad, Lori Gauld, Lori Harding, Lori Jeschke, Luis Saldana, Lynn Field, Lynn Hare, Lynn McGinnis, Madelyn Toliver, Magdy Karam, Marc Hildreth, Marc Hoffman, Marjorie Malpass, Mark Ellis, Mark Lainton, Mark

Reinsbach, Mark Silverman, Mark Skillings, Mary Ann
Rudolph, Mary Kalkanis, Mary Sheldon, Matt Tod, Maya
Razon, McCormac Adam, Megan Pow, Michael Bland,
Michael Leckie, Michael McGuire, Michael Molinaro,
Michelle @ d3design, Michelle Benning, Michelle
McCauley, Mike Olsson, Misha Gloubeman, Morgan
Storie, Nadia Ballantine, Narumi Isoda, Natalie Miller-
Snell, Niamh Hyland, Nicholas Stirling, Nicola Fisher,
Nicole Halton, Nicole Liddell, Nigel Stanier, Noreen
Newton, Ozan Varol, Padraig O'Sullivan, Parham
Doustdar, Paul Allen, Paul Trudel, Pauline Lee, Peter
Howard, Phil Wylie, Prina Shah, Rachael Acello, Rachel
Gorman, Renee Freedman, Rick Brown, Rick Yvanovich,
Robert Whitehouse, Robin Jarvis, Roderic Chabot,
Ronak Sheth, Ruslanas Miliunas, Sacha Luthi, Sandra
L. Schmidt, Sandra Stellhorn, Sanya Ristic, Sarah
Kubicki, Sarah Neumann, Sarah Philp, Scott Sneddon,
Sean Bartman, Shakila Majid, Shannon Minifie, Sharon
Hazard, Shirley Von Sychowski, Shoshana Bloom,
Simon Fletcher, Simon Raby, Sinéad Condon, Soni Basi,
Stanislao Bianchini, Stefan Nemecek, Steinar Hjelle,
Stephanie Hardman, Stephanie McRae, Stephanie
Tower-Doberstein, Steve Morris, Steven D'Souza, Steven
Hermans, Stewart Pollard, Stuart Crabb, Sue Donnelly,

Sue Easby, Susan Bartley, Susan Collett, Susan Lynne, Susie McNamara, Suzanne Schapira, Tammi Jew, Tammy Williams, Tara Deakin, Teri Hassell, Thomas Sebastiao, Thornley Bay, Tiffany Foster Rech, Tina Kao Mylon, Tobin Smith, Toni McLean, Tracy Ferry, Tricia Rolls, Trish Gooch, Uma Santini, Vanessa Le, Victoria Pile, Vipul Malhotra, Vivian Campbell, Whitney Hinshaw Sullivan, and Zsuzsanna O'Neill.

Have the audacity
to dream about
a great working
partnership.

JACQUELINE NOVOGRATZ

About Michael Bungay Stanier

H i, I'm Michael, sometimes called MBS. This is my eighth book. If you know any of my others, most likely it's *The Coaching Habit*, which has sold more than a million copies and is the best-selling book on coaching this century. The one before this one was *How to Begin* (how to set a Worthy Goal as a way of unlocking your own greatness), and back in 2011 I created and edited *End Malaria*, a book I did in partnership with Seth Godin that raised more than $400k for Malaria No More.

I founded Box of Crayons, a learning and development company that's trained lots of people around the world to be more coach-like (BoxOfCrayons.com). Currently much of my attention is given to MBS.works, where we provide people with the resources and community to be better and be a force for change.

Still reading? OK. Other highlights include being happily married for nigh on thirty years, captaining my under-thirteen soccer team, presenting a TEDx Talk that's been seen by about 1.5 million people, being on Brené Brown's podcast, knowing how to make a fair number of great cocktails, being a Rhodes Scholar, being sued by a law professor for defamation, surviving more than twenty Toronto winters, performing in a "nude male modelling" skit in the law revue, playing small roles in inventing stuffed crust pizza and a whisky nominated as "the worst single malt ever invented," and liking my parents, two brothers, and their families.

The best place to get additional resources and information is MBS.works. I'm also on assorted socials: LinkedIn, and @mbs_works for Instagram and Twitter).

Also by Michael Bungay Stanier

How to Begin · 2022
Find your next big thing, something
thrilling, important, and daunting

The Advice Trap · 2020
Tame your Advice Monster so you
can be more coach-like

The Coaching Habit · 2016
The million+ seller that unweirds coaching,
so people can stay curious a little longer

How to Stay Curious Longer

The five questions that lie at the heart of a Keystone Conversation and *How to Work with (Almost) Anyone* ask one big thing from you: to stay curious.

It's not as easy as it sounds. It turns out we're all advice-giving maniacs, and the skill of asking a good question and then being quiet and listening to the answer is tricky.

That's why I wrote *The Advice Trap*. It shows you how to overcome your deeper resistance to staying curious and gets practical about taming your Advice Monster.

Here's the first chapter. You can buy *The Advice Trap* in all the usual places.

P.S. When I coached Brené Brown on her podcast, she called *The Advice Trap* "brilliant."

P.P.S. You can also buy the book and download additional resources at TheAdviceTrap.com.

Easy Change vs. Hard Change

Why it's easy(ish) to figure out your new phone, but hard to keep your resolutions.

Two types of change

Everyone says, "Change is difficult," but honestly, most of the time it's not so bad. You've learned plenty and changed plenty in your life. Figured out how to stream movies and TV shows? Yes, you did. Started a new job, and got the hang of it quickly enough? Of course. A new route to the office, a new skill at work, a new relationship, professional or personal—you started out not knowing, figured it out, practised a bit, got better, and eventually you mastered it. That's Easy Change, and you're pretty good at that.

But there's also Hard Change. No surprise, this is trickier. You've succeeded at Hard Change, but you've also struggled and failed. If you've ever had a New Year's resolution that you keep coming back to and back to and back to... and then back to once more, but *still* can't seem to crack... that's likely a Hard Change challenge. If you keep getting the same feedback in your annual performance review, no matter how hard you try to improve, that's likely a Hard Change challenge.

THE EXPERIENCE OF EASY CHANGE

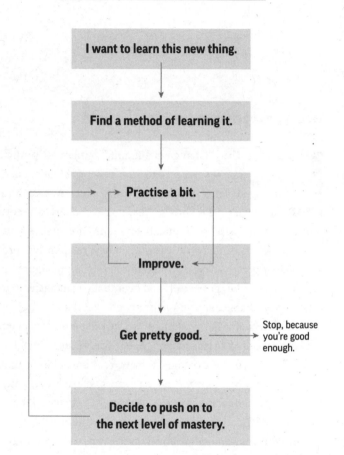

I want to learn this new thing.

Find a method of learning it.

Practise a bit.

Improve.

Get pretty good. → Stop, because you're good enough.

Decide to push on to the next level of mastery.

#TameYourAdviceMonster

THE EXPERIENCE OF HARD CHANGE

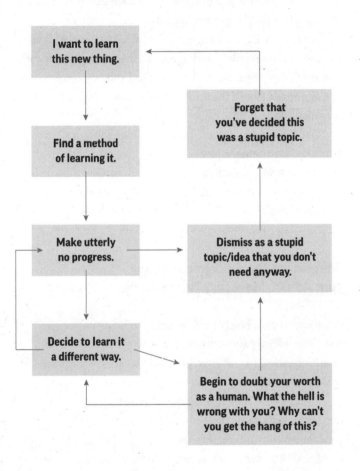

#TameYourAdviceMonster

If you're driving your spouse crazy because you keep doing that thing, even though you don't want to keep doing that thing, that's likely a Hard Change challenge.

The reason Easy Change is fairly straightforward is that you can see the problem and figure out the solution. That solution is additive: figure out what you need and bolt it on to how you're already doing things. It's like downloading a new app on your phone.

Hard Change is more difficult because the Easy Change solutions, frustratingly, just don't work. You've tried them, then tried them again. Downloading the app doesn't work. You just end up with a lot of unused apps. You actually need to install a new operating system.

Being more coach-like and taming your Advice Monster? Hard Change

For a few of you, being more coach-like is Easy Change. I've had those lucky people write to me: "Now that I've read *The Coaching Habit*, I've changed the way I lead. It's a miracle!" I love those emails.

But here's the rub. I also know that the majority don't experience this miracle. It certainly took me time to get it.

Taming your Advice Monster is Hard Change, plain and simple. When something is Hard Change, me giving you my

Hard Change:
You don't
need a new
app; **you
need a new
operating
system**.

best coaching questions doesn't make much of a sustainable difference. Before these tools can become really useful, you have to successfully come to grips with the Hard Change required for you to be more coach-like.

It turns out, it's a battle between Present You and Future You.

Present You vs. Future You: The marshmallow conundrum

Easy Change tinkers with Present You, while Hard Change builds out Future You. It's the adult equivalent of the famous marshmallow test, where children were given one marshmallow and a choice: resist eating it for fifteen minutes and you get a second marshmallow... Future You wins! Alternatively, give in to temptation and Present You gets that one-marshmallow hit... but Future You loses out.

Hard Change involves saying no to some of what's worked so far for Present You. Saying no now enables you to say yes to the promise of future rewards. You're playing a longer-term, harder, bigger game, with a constant temptation to opt out for a

➕

MORE You can read about the recent controversy regarding the marshmallow experiment in the Box of Crayons Lab.

short-term win. You're potentially changing your beliefs and values, roles and relationships, and how you show up in the world.
It's uncomfortable and it's difficult. It's also life-changing.

As you build out Future You, you're going to have setbacks.
Falling back into unhelpful patterns can feel frustrating and a
little embarrassing. After all, it's probably not the first time it's
occurred to you that giving advice isn't always the best form
of leadership. You likely recognized at least one of the three
reasons that advice-giving doesn't work: it's the wrong problem, the wrong solution, and/or the wrong leadership. You
recognize them, because they're part of the way we all work.
The reason they keep showing up as a default way to work is
because Present You (which succumbs to the Advice Monster)
is winning out over Future You (which requires you to stay
curious longer).

Knowing you should be more coach-like is not enough. Being
committed to change is not enough. You need more than insight
and commitment to break patterns and tame your Advice
Monster. That starts by digging into why we like being bad.

The upside of dysfunction

You engage in dysfunctional behaviour because it's not all
downside. You get some sort of benefit from the behaviour, an
immediate small win, even if it's not what you *really* want. It's

a short-term boost for Present You, even as you trade away the bigger win for Future You. These are #WinsNotWins.

The Karpman Drama Triangle (KDT), a model I referenced in *The Coaching Habit*, is a perfect example of that mix of small Present You #WinsNotWins with bigger Future You losses. Stephen Karpman, MD, created the model to explain the dynamics found in Transactional Analysis (TA), a therapeutic approach. The KDT reveals the pattern of three everyday dysfunctional roles: Victim, Persecutor, and Rescuer.

When you're in the KDT and playing one of these roles (and trust me, you've played all of these roles at various times, probably even within the last twenty-four hours), there's a short-term, limited upside and a longer-term downside. Take the Victim role. You pay quite the price: you're stuck, you're powerless, you're whiny, you're sad, you're angry, you're building a reputation you don't want ... and yet the #WinsNotWins are that you're able to blame others for the situation ("they" did it), avoid responsibility, and become the centre of attention to people who love to save Victims.

Or the Persecutor role. Downsides: you're frustrated, angry, shouty, lonely, exhausted, and overwhelmed. The #WinsNotWins are you're able to blame others for things going wrong, feel superior to the turkeys you have to work with, maintain the illusion of control, and be "righteously" angry.

And the Rescuer role, the role most people quickly associate with. The price you pay is significant: you're exhausted, stuck

Build out Future You,

rather than tinkering with Present You.

on an endless treadmill of trying to fix everyone and everything. You're frustrated because you can't get to your own work, as your fingers are in everyone else's pies. To add insult to injury, you perpetuate the KDT by *knowing* people can't do things themselves, thereby creating Victims and Persecutors. The #WinsNotWins? A sense of noble suffering because no one appreciates how you're trying to save the person/situation/team/organization/world, and the pleasure of meddling (in a nice way, of course) in others' business.

The work begins

With #WinsNotWins, you're seeing what my friend Mark Bowden calls the "Prizes & Punishments" in every choice you make. There's always a benefit and there's always a cost. Present You gains short-term benefits from not changing, but misses out on Future You gains. When you take on Hard Change, you're declaring that you choose the bigger, longer-term Prizes you want for Future You.

To become the Future You who values leadership, you need to tame your Advice Monster. That's Hard Change for most of us. The next pages are all about making that Hard Change a little easier.

What was most useful or valuable in this chapter for you?

Before you move on, what are the one or two things you definitely want to remember from this chapter? Writing down the answer increases the likelihood you'll remember it.

....

....

....

....

....

....

....